the Weekend Crafter®

Metal Embossing

the
Weekend
Crafter®

Metal Embossing

20 Simple Projects with Aluminum, Copper & Brass Foils

YOLANDA CARRANZA VALLE

LARK
BOOKS

A Division of Sterling
Publishing Co., Inc.

New York

EDITOR:
MARTHE LE VAN

ART DIRECTOR:
ERIC STEVENS

PHOTOGRAPHY STYLISTS:
STACEY BUDGE
TOM METCALF

COVER DESIGNER:
BARBARA ZARETSKY

ASSISTANT EDITOR:
VERONIKA ALICE GUNTER

PRODUCTION ASSISTANCE:
SHANNON YOKELEY

EDITORIAL ASSISTANT:
DELORES GOSNELL

PHOTOGRAPHER:
EVAN BRAKEN

ILLUSTRATOR:
ORRIN LUNDGREN

PROOFREADER:
SHERRY HAMES

Library of Congress Cataloging-in-Publication Data

Valle, Yolanda Carranza.
    Metal embossing : 20 simple projects in aluminum, copper & brass / Yolanda Carranza Valle.— 1st ed.
        p. cm. — (The weekend crafter)
    Includes index.
    ISBN 1-57990-402-5 (paper)
    1. Embossing (Metal-work) 2. Metal foils. I. Title. II. Series.

    TT205. V297 2003
    745.56—dc21

2002034359

10 9 8 7 6 5 4 3 2 1

First Edition

Published by Lark Books, a division of
Sterling Publishing Co., Inc.
387 Park Avenue South, New York, N.Y. 10016

© 2003, Yolanda Carranza Valle

Distributed in Canada by Sterling Publishing,
c/o Canadian Manda Group, One Atlantic Ave., Suite 105
Toronto, Ontario, Canada M6K 3E7

Distributed in the U.K. by Guild of Master Craftsman Publications Ltd.,
Castle Place, 166 High Street, Lewes, East Sussex, England BN7 1XU.
Tel: (+44) 1273 477374, Fax: (+44) 1273 478606,
Email: pubs@thegmcgroup.com, Web: www.gmcpublications.com

Distributed in Australia by Capricorn Link (Australia) Pty Ltd.,
P.O. Box 704, Windsor, NSW 2756 Australia

If you have questions or comments about this book, please contact:
Lark Books
67 Broadway
Asheville, NC 28801
(828) 236-9730

Printed in China

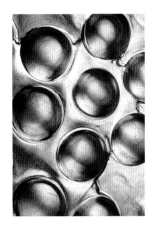

CONTENTS

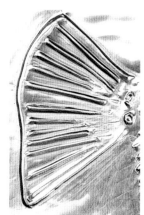
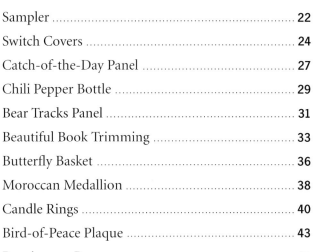

Introduction 6

The Basics 7

    Materials and Tools 7

    Basic Tool Kit 11

    Techniques 12

The Projects

    Sampler 22

    Switch Covers 24

    Catch-of-the-Day Panel 27

    Chili Pepper Bottle 29

    Bear Tracks Panel 31

    Beautiful Book Trimming 33

    Butterfly Basket 36

    Moroccan Medallion 38

    Candle Rings 40

    Bird-of-Peace Plaque 43

    Renaissance Box 45

    On-the-Vine Wine Basket 48

    Fruit-of-the-Earth Journal Cover 50

    Splendor-of-the-Season Watering Can 52

    Wandering Zebras 54

    Macramé Mirror Frame 56

    Aztec Sun Tile 59

    Daisy Chain Frame 62

    Basket of Love 65

Gallery 67

Background Textures 71

Templates 72

About the Author 79

Acknowledgments 79

Notes on Suppliers 79

Index 80

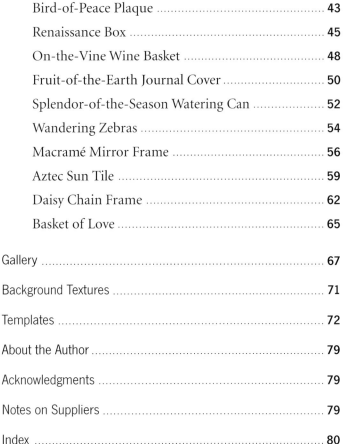

INTRODUCTION

The radiance of metal becomes more enchanting when its surface is embellished with a raised design. This type of decoration is called *embossing*. Metal embossing with foils is an exciting new craft with numerous applications and, above all, exceptionally attractive results. Inspired by the ancient art of repoussé, metal embossing is a fascinating low-tech process that takes advantage of current technology. Modern metal manufacturers have created a pliable type of foil perfectly suited for embossing. Now, beautifully sculpted metal artwork can be an appealing craft technique for everyone to enjoy.

The opening chapter of this book covers metal embossing tools, materials, and basic techniques. Most supplies are easy to find; some you may already have around your home. The more specialized tools and supplies can be purchased at your local crafts, hobby, or art supply store at a small cost. The techniques of metal embossing are not complicated. Once you review the step-by-step basics, you can immediately begin practicing your new skills. Through repetition, the various methods of creating *relief* (the projection of three-dimensional form from a flat background) will become second nature. Your hands will become familiar with the marks of the embossing tools and their capabilities. You will begin to develop an instinctive feel for the metal and a sense of how much pressure to apply to achieve the relief you desire. This special tactile relationship grows stronger over time.

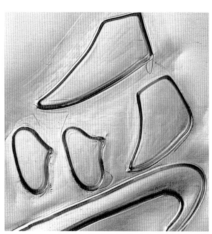

After establishing a working knowledge of the fundamentals of metal embossing, the sky is the limit for its creative application. I have designed a variety of more than 20 projects for you to make, including decorative motifs, floral landscapes, and animal prints. You will have the opportunity to emboss aluminum, copper, and brass. In doing so, you will use different tools and procedures. Once the embossings are complete you can mount them on a variety of surfaces. Keeping with tradition, you can place them in a frame and hang them on the wall, or attach them to wooden plaques. I also have featured some more inventive mounting ideas for you to consider, such as: baskets, watering cans, glass gift bottles, journals, candle rings, tiles, and more.

Because little is written about this craft, most metal embossing artists learn their skills from other individuals. In the beginning, I too sought instruction from experienced artisans. They were more than willing to share their knowledge through show-and-tell demonstrations. After years of personal experience working with tooling foils, I wish to teach you my embossing methods, and I hope you will become similarly enchanted with this art.

THE BASICS

Materials and Tools

Many of the materials and tools used to emboss, or *tool*, metal are common household items. Those materials and tools that you may not have on hand can be easily purchased at craft, discount, or home improvement stores.

Rolled metal tooling foil, from left: brass, copper, aluminum

METAL TOOLING FOILS

These foils are thin enough to be cut with ordinary household scissors. The manufacturer of the metal anneals it specifically for embossing. To *anneal* is to heat and cool the metal in a manner that softens it and makes it less brittle. Craft stores usually sell tooling foils in 9 x 12-inch (22.9 x 30.5 cm) or 12 x 36-inch (30.5 x 91.4 cm) sheets. A variety of metals, including aluminum, copper, and brass, are readily available. Catalog and Internet retailers offer a greater variety in both types and sizes of tooling foil.

Disposable aluminum ovenware is a good substitute to use for practicing metal embossing techniques. Roof flashing, used in home construction, is much thicker. This metal can be embossed, but the techniques and tools are different. Aluminum soft drink cans are not suitable for embossing because they are made of an *alloy*, not pure aluminum, that is too dense to emboss.

METAL FOIL THICKNESS

Metal thickness is measured in several ways. Measurements often differ slightly between metal manufacturers but never enough to affect the embossing projects in this book.

Gauge

Gauges inversely indicate sheet metal's thickness—the higher the gauge number, the thinner the metal. The lightest sheet metal is 30-gauge; material lighter than that is generally categorized as foil. There are two gauge systems with only a slight variation between them. The *American Wire Gauge* (AWG) or *Brown and Sharpe* (B&S) system is used in the United States, while the *British Standard* is common in the United Kingdom. American 36-gauge metal is an insignificant .002 inch (.005 cm) thicker than its British Standard counterpart.

Mils

When foil is measured in thousandths of an inch (2.5 cm), that figure is called *mils*. A piece of 36-gauge metal using the American Wire Gauge (AWG) or Brown and Sharpe (B&S) system is .005 of 1 inch or 5 mils, while a piece of 36-gauge metal using the British Standard is .007 of 1 inch or 7 mils. As you can see, the difference is extremely small.

Metric

The practice of measuring tooling foil in metrics is becoming more widespread. The thickness of a piece of sheet metal is given in fractions of a millimeter. Tooling foils for metal embossing traditionally are either .19 or .12 millimeter.

Common Labels

To further cloud the issue, you may find tooling foil sheets at craft stores labeled only as *medium weight* or *lightweight*. To simplify the different thickness measuring systems, I have used the terms **thick** and **thin** to describe the foils throughout this book. Thick foil is about seven times thicker than regular aluminum food wrap and about four times thicker than heavy-duty food wrapping foil. Thin foil is about half the thickness of the thick foil.

To create the aluminum embossing projects in this book, you will only use thick aluminum foil. Using a thin aluminum foil is not practical. Aluminum is the softest metal foil and is successfully embossed with wooden tools. Copper and brass, both thin and thick, are generally embossed with the same techniques, using both wooden and metal-tipped instruments, although copper is softer than brass.

Use this table as needed to convert the various methods of measurement.

In this book	Thick	Thin
Gauge	36	40
Mils	.005 to .007 of 1 inch	.003 to .005 of 1 inch
Metric	.19 mm	.12 mm
Common	Medium weight	Lightweight

WORK SURFACES

Before you emboss, you will place tooling foil on top of one of five different work surfaces. These range from very hard to very soft depending upon the relief you need to make and the tool and metal you are using. I have determined my favorite work surfaces and listed them below by category. I have also provided alternate surfaces that work equally as well. Feel free to substitute and explore your work surface options.

TRANSFERRING TOOLS

Once you select an embossing project, first you will photocopy the pattern, and then transfer its design onto tracing paper. Use tape to secure the tracing paper in place on the tooling foil, and then retrace the pattern with an empty ballpoint pen or a fine ball stylus.

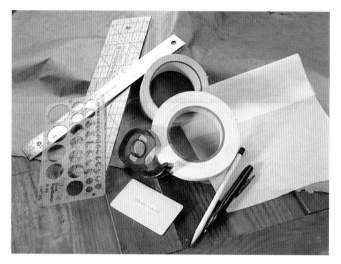

Transferring tools, from left: metal ruler with cork backing, plastic circle template, transparent drafting ruler, plastic card, transparent tape, masking tape, pencil, dry pen, tracing paper

Surface Category

	Very Soft	Soft	Medium	Hard	Very Hard
My Favorite	Foam rubber	Computer mouse pad	Foam place mat	Cardboard (not corrugated)	Glass pane
Alternates	Soft kitchen sponge Folded towel	Layered chamois Layered felt	Craft foam Chamois (single layer) Felt (single layer)	Poster board Food box	Smooth ceramic tile Fiberboard

Very soft embossing surfaces, from left: foam rubber, folded towel, kitchen sponge

Soft embossing surfaces, from left: layered chamois, layered craft foam, layered felt, computer mouse pad

Medium embossing surfaces, clockwise from top: felt, foam place mat, craft foam

Hard embossing surfaces, from left: cardboard, food box

Very hard embossing surfaces, clockwise from left: ceramic tile, fiberboard, glass pane

Assorted coins, bottle lids, and can tops

Other Transfer Tools

A plastic circle template is very handy for drawing and transferring precise curves and circles. Coins, bottle lids, and can tops are also practical guides. Use a plastic card, such as a credit card, to draw and tool small straight lines.

Cutting tools, from left: sharpening stone, craft knife, scissors, decorative-edge scissors

CUTTING TOOLS

Tooling foil is thin enough to be easily cut with a sharp craft knife or scissors. Here are some helpful tips for choosing and maintaining these important tools. (See page 12 for craft knife cutting techniques.)

Craft Knives

A sharp pointed craft knife with changeable blades is a beneficial tool for crafters in any field. A stationary or fixed blade allows you to cut accurate lines down the length of a straightedge, such as a metal ruler. Some metal rulers have a cork backing which will hold the foil down firmly

and keep the straightedge in its intended location. Use a sharpening stone to extend the life of disposable craft knife blades. This frugal yet beneficial practice is described below.

Craft Knife Cutting Surfaces

Always cut tooling foil on some sort of flexible pad. Although flat cardboard makes a good base, metal foil is most easily and smoothly cut on top of a computer mouse pad, a piece of craft foam, or a foam place mat. These bases allow the craft knife to cut downwards as it is moved forward. I have found it a good practice to reserve one pad strictly for cutting foil (you will need others for the actual embossing). Do not use folded newspaper as a base because the foil may shift and cause an accident.

Sharpening Craft Knife Blades

Since metal embossing's most important cutting tool is a craft knife, you will want to maintain a very sharp, straight, pointed, and clean blade. You will have more control with a sharp blade, and your cuts will be more precise. Sharp blades also make cutting safer. With repeated use, a knife blade's point becomes flat, rounded, or otherwise misshapen.

Sharpening a craft knife blade on a lubricated sharpening stone

Instead of frequently replacing the blade, you can sharpen it very quickly and simply. You will need a sharpening stone, also known as an *oilstone*, or a *whetstone*, lubricated with two or

three drops of oil. Firmly hold the knife blade at a very low angle so the beveled cutting edge lies flat against the stone. Move the blade back and forth down the length of the stone. Repeat this process on the reverse side of the blade.

Scissors

Scissors are also indispensable. If possible, have one large-blade and one small-blade pair on hand to tackle any project, from cutting foil to delicate pattern work. Small-blade scissors are especially useful for cutting small indentations near the edge of the tooling foil. Although foil can be cut with utility shears, it is best to use them when precision is not an issue.

EMBOSSING TOOLS

The most unique tools you will use in this craft are the embossing instruments. They stretch and shape the metal foil into relief patterns. Some embossing tools are simple objects you create yourself; some are store bought; and some are everyday items you already may have in your home.

Embossing tools, clockwise from left: narrow-point blending stump, wide-point blending stump, fine-point pencil stylus, broad pencil stylus, extra-broad pencil stylus (all with screwdriver stylus tips on bottom end), narrow-ball metal stylus, medium-ball screwdriver stylus

Wooden Styluses

Prior to embossing metal, you will need to create your own wooden styluses. Fortunately, this is an easy process. First, purchase a long wooden dowel, 5/16 to 3/8 inch (8 to 9.5 mm) in diameter, and cut it into comfortable lengths. My three styluses are each approximately the length of a pen or pencil, from 5 to 7 inches (12.7 to 17.8 cm) long. Next, you will form six ends of the cut dowels into a variety of tip shapes and sizes as described below.

Pencil Styluses

You will make three pencil styluses, each with different points. Create the points by sharpening the end of the wooden dowel with a pencil sharpener, a fine wood file, and/or sandpaper. Make one *fine-point pencil stylus* with an end similar to a dull lead pencil. Also make a *broad pencil stylus*, the end of which resembles a new crayon. Finally, make an *extra-broad pencil stylus* with a more bulbous rounded end.

Screwdriver Styluses

The tip of a screwdriver stylus looks like that of a flathead screwdriver. It has two corners with a flat surface in between. Construct three screwdriver styluses on new wooden dowels, or form them on the opposite end of the pencil styluses. Scrape or sand the end of the dowels with a fine wood file and/or sandpaper to achieve the flathead tip. Finally, file the corners of two screwdriver styluses to construct three sizes of screwdriver heads.

The three distinct areas of the screwdriver stylus' tip work simultaneously. When the stylus is pushed over the foil at an angle, the corner farthest away from the embossed *upfold*, or raised area of the foil, is the leading part. It flattens and smoothes the foil under the stylus. The corner of the stylus nearest the edge of the upfold follows. It sharpens the lower edge of the upfold. The flat center of the stylus sharpens curves. It also levels out nicks in the upfolds and prevents nicks that may otherwise be formed with a pencil stylus.

Metal Ball Stylus

A metal ball stylus is usually a double-ended tool, approximately 5 1/2 inches (14 cm) long. Each ball end is made of stainless steel, treated for hardness, and set in a smooth hardwood handle. Metal ball styluses are essential for embossing harder foils, such as copper and brass. They are often sold in a package that includes narrow-, medium-, and wide-ball ends.

Blending Stumps

Blending stumps are solid, double-ended pointed tools constructed from specially made soft gray paper felt. They are sold in a package that includes narrow-, medium-, and wide-pointed ends. Blending stumps stretch tooling foil gently and smoothly. Always select a blending stump suitable to the size of the area being embossed. You can easily clean and resharpen the ends of blending stumps with sandpaper.

FILLING TOOLS

Once a metal embossing is complete, you will need to construct a firm

Filling tools, clockwise from top left: wood filler, absorbent powder, plastic spatula, plastic palette knife, wooden dowel

foundation to support the relief image. Use wood filler to fill the cavities, or *hollows*, of the raised areas. A small plastic palette knife, spatula, or butter knife is ideal for this task. To soak up moisture from the filler, you will need an absorbent powder, such as baby power, talc, or flour, and tissue paper. Finally, you will use a long wooden dowel of any width, such as a rolling pin, to level the filler.

PATINA SUPPLIES

A *patina* is a mellowed, colored, or aged surface. You can enhance the appearance of embossed metal surfaces by applying special finishes

Patina supplies, clockwise from left: commercial green patina solution, black enamel spray paint, soft cotton cloth, lacquer thinner, paint brushes

known as patinas. This process promotes the contrast of the relief, provides heightened visual drama, or simulates an antique look. You can add a patina to a metal embossing by using chemicals, paint, heat, and oxidation.

Commercial Patina Solutions

Patinas are not simply a paint or faux finish. Commercial patina solutions are chemical formulas that actually cause copper and brass to oxidize as they might naturally through years of weathering. Depending upon their makeup, commercial patinas can produce either green or black tones on metal tooling foil. To achieve the best results and to ensure your personal safety, always follow the manufacturer's directions when using a commercial patina.

Paint Patinas

You can use black enamel paint or black lacquer to colorize reliefs. First, apply the paint with either a spray can or paintbrush. Then, remove the excess color with paint or lacquer thinner and a soft cotton cloth, such as a piece of an old T-shirt. (Textured cloths, such as terry, should not be used; their coarse weaves will remove the paint from the crevices of the embossing.) See page 19 for complete step-by-step directions on how to apply a paint patina.

MOUNTING TOOLS

For some metal embossing projects, the final step is to secure the completed artwork to a surface. The mount must be rigid to support the artwork. You can buy many types of heavy-duty, multipurpose glues that adhere porous and nonporous materials and dry clear. Apply the glue with a small paintbrush or spread it on the back of the artwork with your finger. Use clothespins and/or rubber bands to hold the image to the mount while the glue sets. Once adhered, you can place the embossing over a soft surface, and then place a weight over the artwork until the glue completely dries. A hot-glue gun and hot glue also can be used.

Mounting supplies, clockwise from left: clothespins, heavy-duty multipurpose glue, hot-glue gun, rubber bands

You will use most of the tools on this list to create an embossing project. The list is organized by technique. The items marked "optional" are not required, but they make embossing more accurate and simple to execute.

Transferring Supplies

Tracing paper
Tape
Pencil with eraser
Empty ballpoint pen
Metal ruler (with cork backing if possible)
Plastic circle template (optional)
Assorted coins, jar lids, bottle tops, and other curved objects
Plastic card, such as a credit card

Embossing Supplies

Scissors
Craft knife with blades
Sharpening stone with oil lubricant (optional)
Cutting pad, such as a computer mouse pad, craft foam, or foam place mat
Work surfaces, one of each: very soft, soft, medium, hard, very hard (see page 8 for specific examples)
Wooden pencil styluses, one of each: fine point, broad, extra-broad
Wooden screwdriver stylus
Metal ball styluses, one of each: narrow, medium, and wide
Blending slumps, one of each: narrow, medium, and wide
Sandpaper
Good overhead light

Filling Supplies

Wood filler
Small plastic palette knife, spatula, or butter knife
Absorbent powder, such as baby powder, talc, or flour
Tissue paper
Wooden dowel

Paint Patina Supplies

Black lacquer or enamel paint
Lacquer thinner or paint thinner
Paintbrush (if not using spray paint)
Cotton cloth
Safety glasses
Rubber gloves

Mounting Supplies

Heavy-duty clear-drying glue or hot-glue gun and glue sticks
Clothespins and/or rubber bands
Small paintbrush

Techniques

Soon you will be able to emboss tooling foil with easy-to-use tools and create multi-dimensional images. This section introduces the basic embossing techniques with complete directions in a step-by-step format. I am including hints to help you understand the procedure and to ensure your success. You will apply these basic techniques to each project you make in this book. If you are new to metal embossing, it will be helpful to practice these basic skills.

ONCE YOU BEGIN CREATING PROJECTS, ALWAYS REMEMBER TO EMBOSS FROM THE FOREGROUND TO THE BACKGROUND OF THE DESIGN, AND FROM THE CENTER TO THE EDGES OF THE FOIL, UNLESS OTHERWISE DIRECTED.

CUTTING WITH A CRAFT KNIFE

Hold the craft knife at an angle similar to how you hold a pen or pencil. My experience has shown that if I hold the craft knife (or any type of stylus-type tool) between my index and middle finger I gain more control. This position also places less stress on my hand and fingers.

Always cut toward yourself and press downwards. If you are right-handed, only cut the right-hand side of the foil, and then rotate the image counterclockwise as you work. Left-handed persons should cut the left-hand side of the image and rotate the foil clockwise. This position not only allows a firm grip on the metal with your less dominant hand, but also ensures that the cutting area will remain visible. Rotating the foil is also safer; when you can see the knife blade, accidents are less likely to happen.

Cutting Straight Lines

There are several steps you can take that will result in smooth, straight, and accurate cuts. I suggest using a metal

Using a metal ruler and craft knife on a cutting pad to cut foil in a straight line

ruler with a cork backing to guide the craft knife blade. The cork backing gives traction to the ruler and prevents it from sliding off its intended position. The ruler is made of a hard metal so its edge remains smooth and straight.

Avoid placing the metal ruler directly on top of the line that is to be cut. Instead, determine the thickness of the knife blade and place the ruler away from the line accordingly. Before cutting a line, place the knife blade at two distant points along the ruler's edge to ascertain the precise location of the cut. Once the ruler is correctly positioned, score the metal several times to weaken it at the cut line before fully penetrating the foil.

Cutting Circles and Curves

A plastic circle template is the most effective guide for drawing precise curves. You can use jar lids, can tops, and coins to steer your craft knife as you cut. As with straight lines, score the metal several times to weaken the foil before cutting through it.

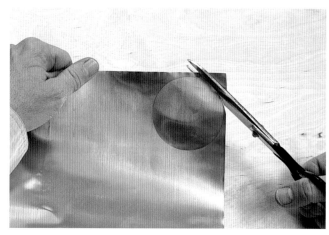

Using scissors to cut a large circle of foil

Small button-size curves (not full circles) are easily cut without scoring. Place the tip of the blade in an upright position at the beginning of the curve. Insert the tip of the point through the foil, and move the blade forward and down around the curve. Very short sawing strokes around larger curves result in cleaner, smoother cuts.

TRANSFERRING A DESIGN

When transferring any design onto metal, conserve as much surface space as possible. Don't start a design in the center of a metal sheet; instead, position the piece near the edge or a corner. You often can use the straight lines of the metal edges to save some extra cutting.

Using Tracing Paper

Place a piece of tracing paper over the photocopied pattern. Use tape to secure the photocopied pattern to the tracing paper and the tracing paper with the design to the metal foil. Use a pencil to trace the design onto the tracing paper. You can easily erase any pencil errors off the tracing paper, and the same sheet can withstand several transfers. Tracing paper also allows the photocopied pattern to be used several times without tearing, and the tape can be easily removed.

YOU WILL NEED
Basic tool kit, page 11
Photocopied pattern of choice
Metal tooling foil

2 Cut a piece of metal tooling foil about 2 inches (5 cm) wider and 2 inches (5 cm) longer than the pattern design requires. (These 1-inch-wide margins will be needed at the start of every project even if they are later removed or if they become part of the background design.) Smooth and flatten the foil as needed with a cotton cloth or with the side of a stylus or stump on top of a very hard work surface (glass pane) as shown.

1 Following the method described above, transfer the photocopied pattern onto the tracing paper.

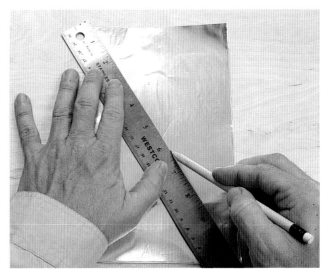

3 Working on the front side of the foil, place a ruler from the upper left corner to the lower right corner. Use a pencil to very lightly draw a line at the center of the ruler. Repeat this process from the other two corners as shown. You now have found the center of the foil.

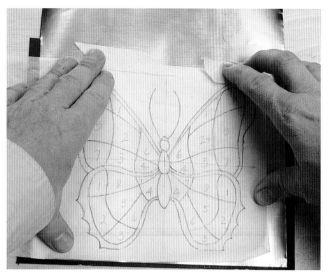

4 Position the center of the pattern over the center of the foil, and level the pattern. Tape the pattern to the front side of the foil as shown.

5 On top of a medium (foam place mat) or hard (cardboard) work surface, trace the pattern onto the foil with an empty ballpoint pen or small ball stylus as shown. Use enough pressure to transfer the pattern clearly without tearing the paper. It may be helpful to use a ruler to draw straight lines and a circle template to draw curves.

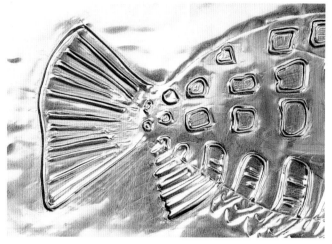

Line relief

LINE RELIEF

Line relief is a narrow embossed line that stands alone or as an outline around another relief form. This line is usually an *upfold*, raised above the surface of the foil.

YOU WILL NEED

Basic tool kit, page 11

Metal tooling foil with transferred pattern, such as Simple Grace Candle Ring, page 75

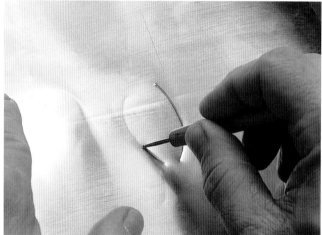

1 Working on the back side of the tooling foil on a soft work surface (computer mouse pad), retrace the transferred pattern lines with enough pressure to emboss the foil. Use a pencil stylus for aluminum foil and a ball stylus for brass or copper. Create any curved pattern lines freehand or by using a circle template. Use a ruler or plastic card as needed to emboss straight lines.

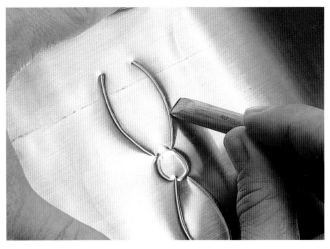

Convex relief

2 Working on the front side of the foil on a very hard work surface (glass pane), smooth the metal surface around the raised lines. Use a blending stump for aluminum and a screwdriver stylus for brass and copper. Start smoothing the foil away from the embossed line, and then move toward the line in a side-to-side "ironing" motion. This ironing process removes imperfections and creates clearer definition between high and low areas. Place the embossed foil on a very hard work surface (glass pane). Enhance the relief between any curved lines and the foil surface with the flat of a screwdriver stylus (see photo). Hold the screwdriver stylus at a 45° angle to the foil and apply a moderate amount of pressure as you drag the stylus toward the relief line.

Concave relief

CONVEX RELIEF

A *convex relief form* is a dome-shape structure that rises from the front side of the metal foil. A *concave relief form* is just the opposite: a crater embossed in the surface of the foil.

YOU WILL NEED
Basic tool kit, page 11
Metal tooling foil with transferred pattern, such as the grapes from On-the-Vine Wine Basket, page 76

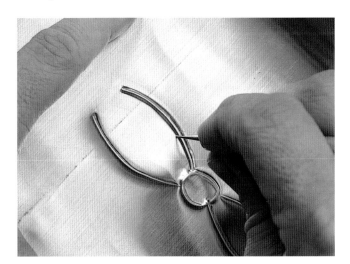

3 Further define embossed lines with a pencil stylus (for aluminum) or a ball stylus (for brass and copper) as shown. Repeat all steps until you achieve the desired level of relief.

1 On a soft work surface (computer mouse pad) retrace the pattern from the back side of the foil with a pencil stylus for aluminum or a ball stylus for brass or copper. Apply enough pressure to emboss the foil.

2 On a soft work surface (computer mouse pad), rub the section to be raised from the back of the foil. Use a blending stump for aluminum. On brass and copper foil use a broad pencil stylus for small areas and a blending stump for large sections. Stroke gently to form the desired shape and height of relief. Add more pressure to areas where greater relief is desired. Gradually lessen the pressure when you sweep across areas of lower relief.

NOTE

If there are several convex relief areas in a design, fully emboss and define the item at the foreground first completing steps 2 and 3; then finish the item on the next level using the same process, and so on until all convex forms are created.

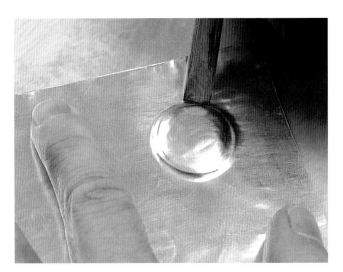

3 Working from the front side of the foil on a very hard work surface (glass pane), use the flat of a screwdriver stylus for aluminum or a small ball stylus for brass and copper to define the edges and emphasize the relief of the convex form. Apply enough pressure to sharpen the shape at its perimeter.

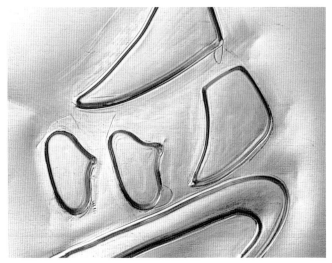

Flat relief

FLAT RELIEF

Like convex relief, flat relief is characterized by a broad elevated surface. However, the raised surface is flat and parallel to the work surface, not curved or domed. The vertical walls of a flat relief are at a 90° angle to both the upper and lower surfaces of the foil.

YOU WILL NEED

Basic tool kit, page 11

Metal tooling foil with transferred pattern, such as the Asian character from Basket of Love, page 78

1 Retrace the pattern from the back side of the tooling foil over a soft work surface (computer mouse pad). Use a pencil stylus for aluminum and a ball stylus for brass or copper. Apply enough pressure to emboss the foil.

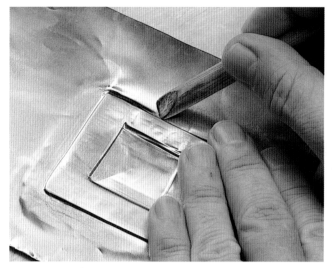

2 Working from the back side of the foil on a soft work surface (computer mouse pad), uniformly increase the amount of relief throughout the pattern area. Use a blending stump or screwdriver stylus for aluminum or an extra-broad pencil or screwdriver stylus for brass and copper.

4 Repeat the ironing process this time on the background of the design from the front side of the foil. Start away from the flat relief area, and iron toward the walls. Use a screwdriver stylus to enhance the corners. Repeat steps 2 through 4 until you achieve the desired amount of relief.

HINTS

- Placing a light source directly above the embossed foil causes the flat relief to cast shadows. Narrow shadows cast by the walls indicate that 90° angles have been achieved.

- The more tooling foil is worked, the thinner it becomes. Take care to avoid tearing the foil. If a tear occurs on the edge of a relief form there is a remedy. Simply close the gap; it probably will not show once the filler and patina are added.

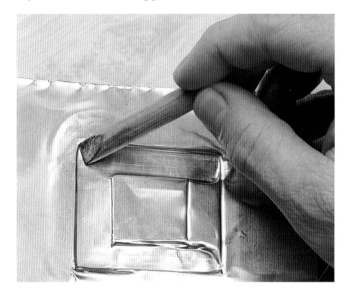

3 Working on the back side of the foil on a very hard work surface (glass pane), "iron" the design from the center, or *floor*, to the raised sides, or *walls*. This process removes bubbles and imperfections and creates greater contrast between the high and low relief areas. Slide a screwdriver stylus to form sharp corners between the walls and the floor. (Remember to hold the screwdriver stylus at a 45° angle to the foil.)

BACKGROUND RELIEF

You can texturize the background of a metal embossing either before or after filling its hollows. Select any background you enjoy; this can be a very simple linework or an ornate decorative pattern. Working on a softer surface produces a background texture with a higher and more pronounced relief. A harder work surface results in a lower, more subtle texture.

YOU WILL NEED

Basic tool kit, page 11

Metal tooling foil with any embossed design

1 Select a background design from page 71, or create your own motif. Place the foil face up on a medium (foam place mat) or hard (cardboard) work surface. (Most background designs are embossed from the front side of the foil.)

2 Emboss the background design on a medium (foam place mat) or hard (cardboard) work surface.

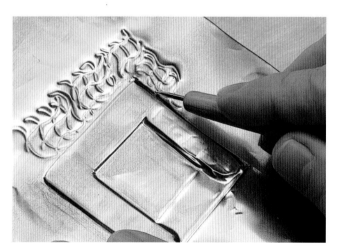

3 Working on the front side of the foil on a very hard work surface (glass pane), outline the boundary between the background texture and the embossed image. Use a pencil stylus for aluminum and a ball stylus for brass and copper.

FILLING THE HOLLOWS

After embossing the foil, you will fill the hollows on the back side of the artwork with wood filler to give support to the raised areas. Carefully, correctly, and cleanly filling the hollows results in a higher quality embossing. On some occasions, however, thick brass and copper foil designs will not require filling. Always refer to the project instructions.

YOU WILL NEED

Basic tool kit, page 11

Metal tooling foil with any embossed design

Hair dryer (optional)

1 Place the embossed foil face down on a very soft (foam rubber) or soft (computer mouse pad) work surface or hold the embossing in your hand. Use a small plastic palette knife, spatula, or butter knife to fill the hollows with the wood filler as shown. It may be helpful to use the wall of the hollow to scrape the filler off the spatula, and then fill the center. (If the background design is in low relief, it will not need filling. A background in high relief, especially on aluminum, may require support.) Do not fill embossed areas that will be cut out. Remove all excess wood filler by scraping and/or wiping it off with a damp cloth. Rub off small amounts of dry filler with a blending stump.

2 Use the spatula to level the wood filler to the height of the background. Sprinkle the surface of the filler with an absorbent powder such as baby powder, talc, or flour. Pat the filler to remove air bubbles. Cover the filled area with a layer of tissue paper. Roll a dowel over the paper to level the filler (see photo). Remove the paper. If more filler is needed, repeat steps 1 and 2. (Don't worry if the filler shows your fingerprints.)

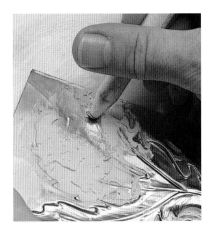

3 Use the blending stump to remove any filler that overflowed its borders. Once the overflow is removed, the outline of each raised design will be clearly visible. Clean the borders with a damp cloth.

4 Set the embossing aside to dry on a soft surface. The drying time of the filler varies depending upon air temperature, humidity, and the depth of the hollows. You can speed the drying time by using a hair dryer or by placing the embossing near a radiator vent or outdoors. The filler is dry when it becomes hard. Test for hardness at the point with the deepest filler. Repeat steps 1 through 4 to refill any shrunken or cracked areas in the dried wood filler (see photo).

APPLYING A PAINT PATINA

Use a paint patina when you want to create a more dramatic embossing. The addition of a color that contrasts in appearance with the metallic tooling foil enhances the depth of the relief.

1 Working outdoors or in a well-ventilated area, prepare the black lacquer or enamel paint for use following the manufacturer's instructions. Brush or spray the paint on the foil to cover all the downfolds and the embossed background of the design. (Painting beyond these areas is not a problem.) Allow the paint to dry only to the touch; a longer drying time makes the removal of excess paint more difficult.

2 To remove the excess lacquer or enamel paint, first wad a soft cotton cloth into a tight bundle, or wrap the cloth around your index finger. (A taut cloth ensures the paint is only removed from the high relief areas.) Dab a small amount of the lacquer or paint thinner onto the cloth. Using long strokes, rub across the entire painted metal embossing as shown. Remove as little or as much of the paint as you desire.

MOUNTING WITH ADHESIVES

You can mount metal embossings on a variety of surfaces. One important consideration is the material you will use to secure the artwork to its mount. If you plan to glue your embossing, choose a heavy-duty fixative that can bond metal to porous and nonporous materials. There are many alternatives to glue mounting, for example the Basket of Love on page 65 uses brass brads.

2 Place the metal embossing on the mounting surface and rub the background down with a blending stump or with your finger. Clean off any excess glue from the surface with a damp cloth.

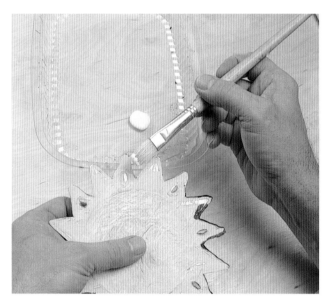

1 Determine where on the mounting surface you wish to adhere the completed metal embossing. Use a paintbrush or your finger to carefully apply a thin and even coat of glue to the back side of the embossing. (Excess glue may ooze out from under the metal, marring the surface even though it dries clear.)

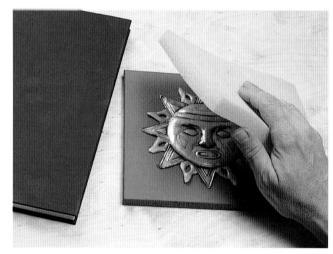

3 Use one of the following three methods to secure the metal embossing to the mounting surface until the glue dries: clip several clothespins near the edges of the embossing to hold the two surfaces together; wrap several strong rubber bands around the entire piece; or place a piece of very soft foam rubber on top of the mounted embossing as shown, and then put a weight over the foam.

I recommend wearing safety glasses and gloves, especially when you are working with patina supplies. Use enamels, lacquers, and thinners outside if possible or in well-ventilated areas.

Having sufficient overhead lighting is important to metal embossing. The shadows a good light creates will help to clarify a shape's contour and the amount of relief being achieved.

To make styluses more comfortable to hold, add padding or several layers of duct tape around the dowel.

Hold the craft knife and styluses correctly to prevent hand cramps (see Cutting with a Craft Knife, page 12).

REPOUSSÉ

Repoussé, the classical means of embossing metal through hammering and annealing, is an ancient art, dating back almost as far as metalsmithing itself. A tradition in almost every corner of the world, repoussé was used to create many forms such as decorative architectural reliefs, vessels, arms and armature, jewelry, and more. It is also famous for its use in religious art.

Repoussé techniques may date back to the Bronze Age (2800–1100 B.C.). Western masterpieces have been discovered from the ancient civilizations of Italy, Assyria, Greece, and Phoenicia. Celtic repoussé ornaments have been found that date from the decline of the Roman Empire (300–600 A.D.) until the Middle Ages (A.D. 5th to 15th century). During the Italian Renaissance (early 14th to late 16th century) repoussé became intensely popular, and the technical peak of the art was reached.

History reveals that Europe was not the only country to practice this ancient art form. In the western hemisphere the art of repoussé first began in South America, where there were rich deposits of gold, silver, and copper. One of the earliest pieces of hammered gold, dating from 1500 B.C., was discovered in the Peruvian highlands. Artists in Asia, especially in Nepal, China, and Afghanistan, used repoussé to create temple sculptures, religious figurines, and architectural details.

Alexander Petrie. *Coffee pot,* circa 1750-1760. Silver; chased and raised decoration. Collection of the Museum of Early Southern Decorative Arts.

One of the largest and most famous repoussé sculptures in the world can be found on Liberty Island in the New York City harbor. *Liberty Enlightening the World,* better known as the Statue of Liberty, was sculpted by Auguste Bartholdi. Gustave Eiffel was the project's structural engineer. This commanding repoussé was presented to America by the people of France on July 4, 1884.

Frederic Auguste Bartholdi. *Liberty Enlightening the World,* 1884. Copper. By Courtesy of the Statue of Liberty Monument.

THE PROJECTS

Sampler

A sampler can be many things — a box of candy filled with a variety of sweet treats or an embroidered design with letters and words sewn in a variety of stitches. Because it includes all the basic techniques of metal embossing, this project is my own version of a sampler.

YOU WILL NEED

Basic tool kit, page 11

Traced pattern, page 72

Aluminum tooling foil,
6 1/4 x 7 3/4 inches
(15.9 x 19.7 cm), plus
1-inch-wide (2.5 cm) margins

TECHNIQUES

Cutting, page 12

Transferring, page 13

Line relief, page 14

Convex relief, page 15

Flat relief, page 16

Background relief, page 18

Filling hollows, page 18

Applying a paint patina,
page 19

Mounting, page 20 (optional)

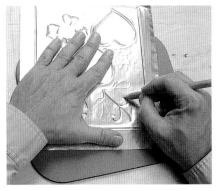

1 Center and transfer the pattern onto the aluminum tooling foil. Emboss the border, the flower stems, and the outline of the middle and lower hearts in line relief as shown.

2 Emboss the flowers in convex relief. Emboss the lower heart in double relief as shown. (A convex relief outlined by a line relief is called a *double relief*.)

3 Emboss the sections of the top heart in flat relief as shown.

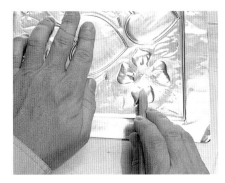

4 To taper the points of the stem tips (see pattern, 1) work from the front side of the foil on a very hard work surface (glass pane). Place the screwdriver stylus at an angle at the end of the stem. Push the stylus toward the line to form a point. Repeat this process on the other side of the same stem to make an arrow-tip point. To make flower petal creases, place a pencil stylus on the dot located at the base of each petal (see pattern, 2). Slowly lower the stylus onto the convex petal as shown.

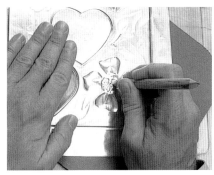

5 To create a stone-like texture in the sections of the upper heart (see pattern, 3), work from the back side of the foil on a soft work surface (computer mouse pad) and lightly draw random short wavy lines. To form tiny buds (see pattern, 4) work on the back side of the foil on a soft work surface (computer mouse pad). Use a pencil stylus to make large dots. First outline the dots from the front side of the foil with a screwdriver stylus, and then with a small ball stylus. To emboss the leaf veins (pattern, 5) work on the back side of the foil on a medium work surface (foam place mat). Emboss the vein lines from the center of the leaf to its edge. If you wish to create a jagged-edge leaf, work on the front side of the foil on a very hard work surface (glass pane) and push the edges between the vein lines with the corner of a screwdriver stylus. To create the flower center (pattern, 6) work on the back side of the foil on top of a soft work surface (computer mouse pad). Use a pencil stylus and randomly tap at the flower center (see photo, lower center column). Tap more in the middle to raise the relief at that point.

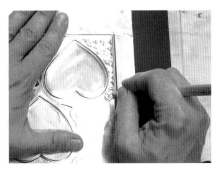

6 Add a background (see photo). Choose any background pattern you wish or design your own motif (see page 71 for examples).

7 Fill the hollows. Use a craft knife to cut out the area of the middle heart within the relief line as shown. Apply a black paint patina. Place a favorite photo under the cutout heart, and frame the sampler as desired.

Switch Covers

Add a unique touch to your interior design with these embossed switch and socket covers. Whether you choose the floral, animal, or graphic motif, many embossing techniques will come into play. These small projects can be created in an afternoon, and make great gifts.

Design: Spring

YOU WILL NEED

Basic tool kit, page 11

Aluminum or thin brass tooling foil,
3 ¹/₂ x 5 ¹/₂ inches (8.9 x 14 cm)

Traced base template,
decorator or toggle, page 72

Light switch plate

Traced pattern of your
choice, pages 72 and 73

Paring knife (Lace design only)

TECHNIQUES

Cutting, page 12

Transferring, page 13

Line relief, page 14 (Desert Friends,
Spring, Lace, Harvest, Hunter's Pride)

Convex relief, page 15 (Desert Friends,
Spring, Harvest, Hunter's Pride)

Flat relief, page 16
(Harvest and Hunter's Pride)

Background relief, page 18

Filling hollows, page 18

Applying a paint patina, page 19

Designs, left to right: Hunter's Pride, Harvest, Lace

BEFORE YOU BEGIN

Please note the following symbols and their meanings when working with the templates on page 72 and 73.

Dotted lines indicate the location of the switch opening.

Dash lines indicate the fold line of the foil.

Circles with intersecting lines indicate the location of the plate's screw holes.

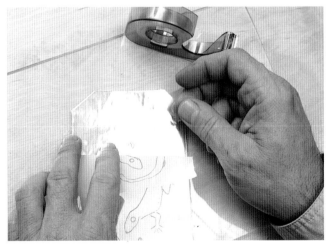

1 Cut the foil as the base template and mark the screw hole locations from the light switch plate. Match the screw symbols on the pattern to those marked on the foil (see photo). Transfer the pattern onto the foil.

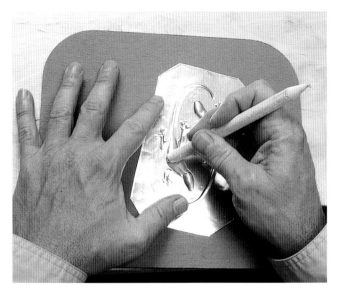

2 Emboss the foil using the following techniques for your selected pattern.

Desert Friends
Emboss the lizard bodies in convex relief as shown. Emboss the lizard toes in line relief.

Spring
Emboss the flower petals and round flower centers in convex relief. Retrace the petal lines with a pencil stylus from the front side of the foil.

Lace
Emboss the stems in line relief. To create the small leaves, use a pencil stylus on the back side of the foil over a medium work surface (foam place mat). Emboss a ¼-inch (6 mm) line, and then curve the line back to the beginning point without raising the stylus. Outline the small leaves from the front side of the foil on a very hard work surface (glass pane). To imprint a leaf vein, lower the point of the paring knife on the pointed end of the leaf.

Harvest
Emboss the small wheat centers in convex relief. Emboss the wheat bristles in line relief. To create the flat leaves at the top and sides of the pattern, emboss the shapes in flat relief. Draw the leaf veins with an empty ballpoint pen from the front side of the foil.

Hunter's Pride
Emboss all pointed and rounded shapes in convex relief; all square shapes in flat relief; and all narrow lines in line relief.

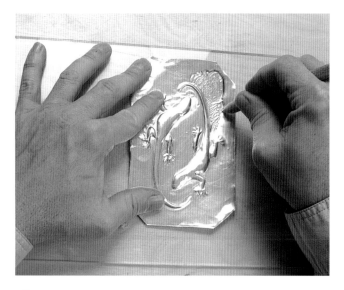

3 From the front side of the foil, add a low background texture of your choice as shown, but keep the foil at the plate openings flat. Fill the hollows. Add a patina if desired.

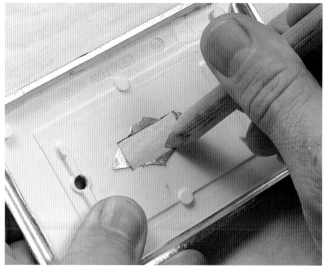

5 Use a craft knife to slit the foil over the switch opening from corner to corner. Fold the sections of slit foil to the back side of the plate and trim. Smooth down the foil-covered openings with a screwdriver stylus (see photo).

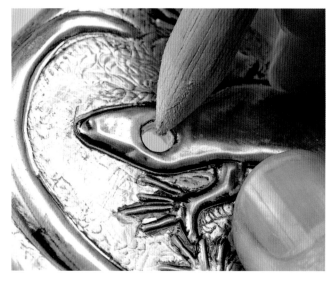

4 Brush the glue on the plate and adhere the embossed foil. Perforate the foil over the screw holes. Swivel a pencil stylus into the perforations to mold the foil to the plate as shown. Smooth down the foil background with a blending stump to remove air pockets and to locate the switch openings. Outline the design again as needed with a ball stylus.

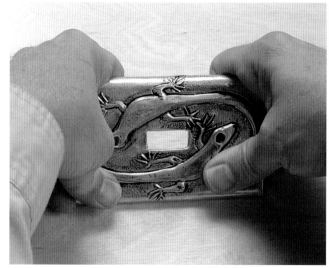

6 Firmly hold the foil and plate combination face down and neatly fold the edges of the foil. On a very hard work surface, slowly drag and turn the plate around to the back as shown. Wrap and mold the excess foil to fit the contour of the back of the plate with a stump or stylus. Repeat this process on the opposite side of the plate, and then on all remaining sides. Trim and tap the foil-covered corners of the plate on a very hard work surface (glass pane) to make them smooth.

Catch-of-the-Day Panel

Fish species exist from the Polar regions through the tropics, in deep oceans and tiny brooks. Nearly as adaptable, this pattern can be used in many different ways. The two fish can be transferred onto a single piece of foil, embossed on separate sheets, or featured individually. You can arrange them vertically as shown, or have them swimming horizontally in an underwater scene.

1 Position the pattern on the foil in a pleasing way, and transfer the design.

  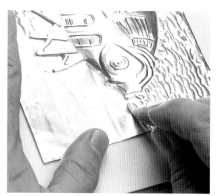

2 Emboss the fishing line, and then the fins, eyes, and mouths in line relief. Use the same technique to outline the spots of Fish 1 (see photo) and the gill-tail line on Fish 2. Emboss the remaining fins and both fish tails.

4 Work from the back side of the foil over a soft work surface (computer mouse pad). Hold the pencil stylus at a very low angle to make the scales on Fish 2 (see photo). The placement and size of the scales are up to you. Outline the curve of each scale from the front of the foil with a small ball stylus.

6 From the front side of the foil use a fine-point pencil stylus to draw a background pattern of closely packed waves or any other texture you wish.

3 From the back side of the foil use blending stumps to form the layers of the fish faces in convex relief as shown. Working over a very hard work surface (glass pane), define the layers of the face from the front side of the foil with a fine-point pencil stylus.

5 Contour each fish body in convex relief from the back side of the foil. Use a broad blending stump or a wadded cloth over very soft work surface (foam rubber) as shown. Use a pencil stylus to outline the entire fish from the front side of the foil over a very hard work surface (glass pane). Repeat this process until you achieve the desired amount of relief.

7 Fill the hollows. Refill the hollows to the level of the background after the first application dries (see photo). Apply a paint patina. Mount or frame the panel as you wish. (I chose a wooden frame with an antique blue finish, hammered a rusty nail on each side, and hung two coordinating fishing bobs to enhance the rustic style.)

Chili Pepper Bottle

Many people are making their own flavored oils and vinegars and storing them in bottles. Decorating these bottles and their caps is a great way for the conscientious crafter to refashion and recycle. The cut-out chili peppers in this design let the bottle's colorful contents show through the embossed foil.

YOU WILL NEED

Basic tool kit, page 11

Traced patterns A, B, and C, page 73

2 aluminum tooling foil strips, each 1 x 5 inches (2.5 x 12.7 cm)

Aluminum tooling foil strip, 3 x 11 inches (7.6 x 27.9 cm)

Aluminum tooling foil square, 2 x 2 inches (5 x 5 cm) for cap top

Glass bottle with cap

Pinking shears

Measuring tape

TECHNIQUES

Cutting, page 12

Transferring, page 13

Line relief, page 14

Convex relief, page 15

Filling hollows, page 18

Applying a paint patina, page 19

NOTE:
Pattern B, repeated once, fits a bottle with a 3-inch (7.6 cm) diameter. The circumference of the bottle is approximately 10 inches (25.4 cm).

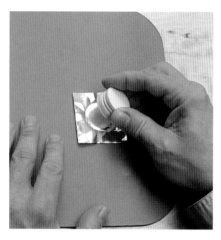

1 Transfer pattern A onto both 1 x 5-inch (2.5 x 12.7 cm) strips of aluminum tooling foil. Transfer pattern B onto the 3 x 11-inch (7.6 x 27.9 cm) foil strip, repeating the pattern at the dots. Imprint the bottle cap opening in the center of the 2 x 2-inch (5 x 5 cm) square as shown, and then transfer pattern C onto the foil.

2 Emboss the narrow foil strips in line relief. Tool the dots. Draw closely packed lines on a very hard work surface (glass pane) to lower the background as shown.

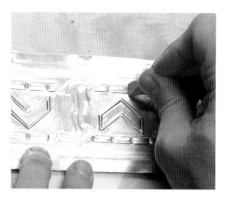

3 Outline the V-shapes on the wide foil strip in line relief. Emboss each horizontal bar as one piece. On a very hard work surface (glass pane), lower a screwdriver stylus on the vertical pattern lines to divide the bars (see photo). Emboss the pepper stems in line relief. Fill the background with dots tooled from both the front and back sides.

4 Use convex relief to form the chili pepper in the center of the cap foil square (see photo). Emboss the pepper's stem and lines. Lower the background as done in step 2.

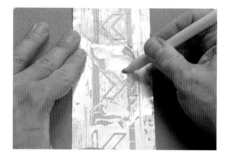

5 Fill the hollows of all embossed foil, let dry, and then clean off any excess filler as shown. Apply a paint patina.

6 Cut out the foil areas as indicated by the shading on pattern B. Trim the wide strip with pinking shears. Measure the height of the cap and trim one of the narrow strips to fit this dimension. Cut the margins off the other narrow strip. Use pinking shears to trim off about 1/8 inch (3 mm) from the outer edge of the embossed bottle cap as shown.

7 Apply glue to the wide embossed strip, and then smooth the strip onto the bottle with a blending stump. Trim the length of the strip as needed. Use rubber bands to hold the strip in place while the glue dries. Mount and trim the neck band. Clip the round piece between the points to the circle, and adhere the foil to the bottle cap. Holding them firmly together over a very hard work surface (glass pane), drag and turn the points around to mold the foil edges to the cap wall. Mount and trim the narrow band around the bottle cap as shown. After the glue dries, scrape any excess off the glass with a craft knife.

Bear Tracks Panel

This pattern is based on real bear tracks which indent into the ground.
The paw prints are made using concave relief with convex shapes at the center.
Adding a strong black patina inside the prints enhances their graphic character.

YOU WILL NEED

Basic tool kit, page 11

Aluminum tooling foil, 3 1/2 x 10 1/4 inches (8.9 x 26 cm) plus 1-inch-wide (2.5 cm) margins

Yard or meter ruler

Traced pattern, page 74

Wood plaque, painted if desired

Hot-glue gun and glue stick

Decorative metal studs (optional)

Hammer (optional)

Large turquoise beads (optional)

TECHNIQUES

Cutting, page 12

Transferring, page 13

Line relief, page 14

Convex relief, page 15

Concave relief, page 15

Filling hollows, page 18

Applying a paint patina, page 19

Mounting, page 20

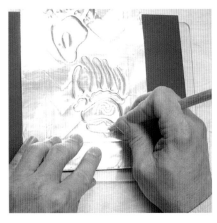

1 Find the center of the aluminum tooling foil with a yard or meter ruler. Transfer the pattern onto the tooling foil. Working from the front side of the foil on a hard work surface (cardboard), use a pencil stylus to outline the outer boundary of each section of the paw prints as shown.

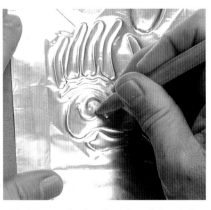

2 From the back side of the foil, emboss the center sections of each paw print in convex relief, but do not outline these center sections. Emboss the remainder of the paw print from the front for a concave relief (see photo) so the foil curves down instead of up.

3 From the back side of the foil, smooth every other chevron stripe with a blending stump over a very hard work surface (glass pane). Repeat this process on the other stripes from the front side of the foil as shown. To keep the background subtle, do not sharpen the edges of the chevrons.

4 From the back side of the foil on a soft work surface (computer mouse pad) use a pencil stylus and a ruler to score the straight line border of the design. Hold the ruler on a scored edge, and fold the foil edge up to form one side of a box as shown. (The fold will not be perfectly straight.) Repeat this process on the other scored edges. Pinch together the corners of the folded edges to join the sides of the box. Define the edges around the inside of the box with a pencil stylus.

5 Slowly add water to the wood filler and stir until it reaches the consistency of cake batter. Pour the wood filler into the foil box to cover the bear tracks (see photo). To remove air bubbles from the filler, carefully drop the artwork from a height of about 6 inches (15.2 cm) onto a level, padded surface. Repeat this action several times. Allow the wood filler to dry thoroughly.

6 Fold the side edges of the foil box over the dried filler as shown. Cut the corners as needed to make the folding neater and easier. Apply a paint patina to the embossed surface, and then hot glue the artwork to a wood plaque. Hammer decorative metal studs to the board if desired. Use hot glue to adhere turquoise beads between the studs if you wish.

Beautiful Book Trimming

By enhancing your plain photo albums and scrapbooks with an elegant embossed medallion and book corners, you can remember and honor your loved ones in style. Any hardback book, even one with a padded cover, can be embellished. Using copper and brass gives the design an antique look, making the project an instant heirloom.

YOU WILL NEED

Basic tool kit, page 11

4 thick copper tooling foil pieces, each
3 3/4 x 1 1/2 inches (9.5 x 3.8 cm)

Transparent drafting ruler

Traced patterns A and B, page 74

Thick copper tooling foil, 3 x 4 1/4
inches (7.6 x 10.8 cm) plus
1-inch-wide (2.5 cm) margins

Decorator scissors or pinking shears

4 thick brass tooling foil strips,
each 1 x 4 inches (2.5 x 10.2 cm)

Thick brass tooling foil strip,
1 inch (2.5 cm) x length of album
or book + 1 inch (2.5 cm)

Photo album or book

TECHNIQUES

Cutting, page 12

Transferring, page 13

Line relief, page 14

Convex relief, page 15

Background relief, page 18

Filling hollows, page 18

Applying a paint patina, page 19

Mounting, page 20

1 Work on the 3 3/4-inch (9.5 cm) side of one small copper foil piece over a soft work surface (computer mouse pad). Position the transparent drafting ruler 1/8 inch (3 mm) in from the edge of the foil. With a small ball stylus use pressure to draw a line on the foil down the straight edge. Keeping the ruler in place, run the point of the stylus under the edge of the foil to begin a fold (see photo). Complete the fold, and then repeat this process on the other three small copper pieces.

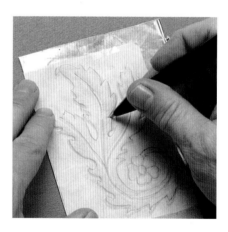

2 Transfer pattern A (medallion design) onto the larger copper foil piece as shown. Transfer pattern B (single flower design) on two of the four small copper foil pieces.

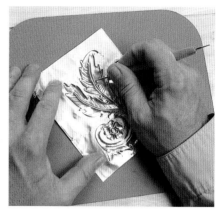

3 Emboss the primary leaf veins of the medallion design in line relief. Raise the relief of the leaf and all the flowers in convex relief. Add texture to the leaf from the back side of the foil. Gently tool minor veins at an angle from the primary vein to the edge of the leaf (see photo). Apply a background design to the four book corners. Fill all hollows. Apply a patina if desired.

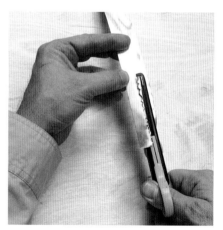

4 Cut out the medallion. Place the embossing face up on a hard work surface (cardboard). Rub the cut edges under with an upright ball stylus. Mark a guideline along the length of each brass strip, 1/2 inch (1.3 cm) in from one edge. Cut along the guideline with decorator scissors or pinking shears as shown.

5 Fold one small embossed copper piece around one book corner until two edges of the foil meet in the back (see photo). Smooth and flatten the foil book corner. Remove it from the book, and trim the length of the back foil flaps to match the length of the front. Repeat this process on the other three corner pieces. Remember to use the two flower-patterned copper pieces on the front book corners and the other two copper pieces in the rear.

7 Evenly brush a layer of glue onto all the foil pieces. Adhere the long strip of brass foil on the left side of the front cover with its decorative edge facing the book's spine. Fold the excess foil under the flap of the book, and hold the ends down with clothespins to dry. Glue the book corners in position, with the decorative edge of the short brass strips underneath as shown. Tap the foil book corners on a very hard work surface (glass pane) to remove sharp points. Center and affix the embossed foil medallion to the front cover of the book. Place a piece of soft foam, and then a heavy book over the medallion until the glue dries.

6 Measure the length of the book corner from fold to fold, and add 1/2 inch (1.3 cm). Cut a small brass foil strip to this measurement. (About 1/4 inch [6 mm] of this decorative edge will extend beyond the book corners.) Trim the ends of the strip at an angle to fit the book corner (see photo). Repeat this process to make a brass strip to fit between the other book corners.

Butterfly Basket

The butterfly is a thrilling feast for the eyes, a natural and inspiring mosaic of color, form, and texture. It is also an important symbol of renewal and rebirth. In this pattern I have provided you with open wings on which to emboss the backgrounds of your choice and to capture the essence of the butterfly.

YOU WILL NEED

Basic tool kit, page 11

Traced pattern, page 74

Aluminum tooling foil, 6 $\frac{1}{4}$ x 5 $\frac{3}{4}$ inches (15.9 x 14.6 cm) plus 1-inch-wide (2.5 cm) margins

TECHNIQUES

Cutting, page 12

Transferring, page 13

Line relief, page 14

Convex relief, page 15

Flat relief, page 16

Background relief, page 18

Filling hollows, page 18

Applying a paint patina, page 19

Mounting, page 20

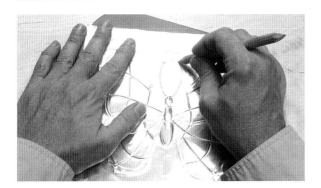

1 Transfer the pattern onto the aluminum tooling foil. Emboss the butterfly's antennae and wing divisions in line relief. Emboss a dot at the tip of each antenna (see photo).

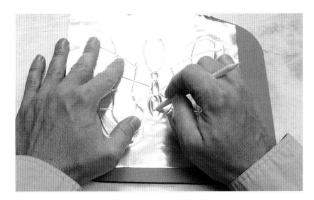

2 Contour and structure the butterfly's body in convex relief.

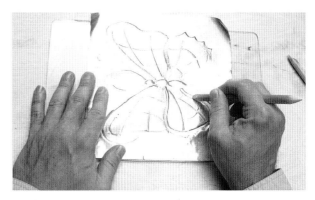

3 Emboss the outer edges of the butterfly wings in flat relief.

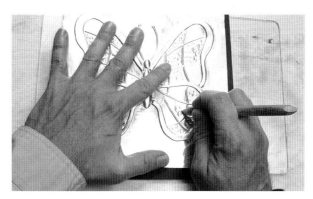

4 From the front side of the foil, fill the wing sections with various background textures as shown. (The numbers on the butterfly pattern refer to the specific background textures found on page 71.) Use both a pencil stylus and a ball stylus to create the background designs.

5 Use the linen pattern on page 71 to texturize the butterfly's background area as shown. While applying the background, spread your hand over the foil to keep it from curling. Fill the hollows of the butterfly body and the outer edges of its wings. Apply a black paint patina to the embossing, and then mount it as desired. (I glued my embossing to the slightly curved side of a contemporary plastic container.)

Moroccan Medallion

This pattern is influenced by ornate North African tile work where shapes unfurl symmetrically from a central point. Embossing the design lets smooth convex forms project above the surface like miniature domes. These are intensified with a double relief. You will enjoy contouring the metal and adding texture to this handsome embossing.

YOU WILL NEED

Basic tool kit, page 11

Traced pattern, page 75

Aluminum tooling foil,
6 x 6 inches (15.2 x 15.2 cm) plus 1-inch-wide (2.5 cm) margins

Plastic circle template or coins and shirt buttons

TECHNIQUES

Cutting, page 12

Transferring, page 13

Line relief, page 14

Convex relief, page 15

Filling hollows, page 18

Background relief, page 18

Applying a paint patina, page 19

Mounting, page 20

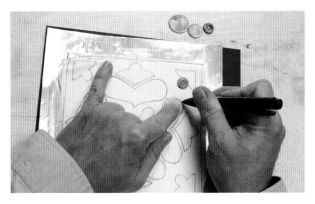

1 Transfer the pattern onto the foil. Use a plastic circle template, coins, or shirt buttons as needed to help make the curved lines. (Even if the objects are not the same size as the curve, they will help guide the stylus as shown.) Use a ruler or a plastic card to help transfer the straight lines.

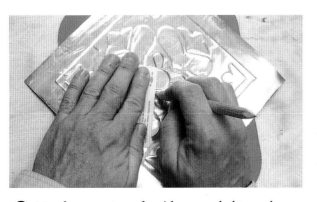

2 Use the same transfer aids as needed to emboss the entire pattern in line relief (see photo). From the front side of the foil, smooth the rest of the surface area flat with a blending stump.

3 Emboss the center of each shape in convex relief. Periodically redefine the margins between the convex and line-relief structures by retracing the margins with a fine pencil stylus over a very hard work surface (glass pane) as shown. This technique, adding a convex relief inside a line relief, is called *double relief.*

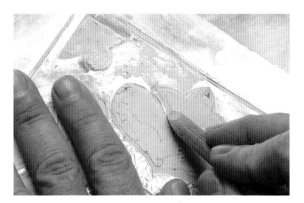

4 Fill the hollows. Use a screwdriver stylus to scrape filler off the margins between line relief and convex structures.

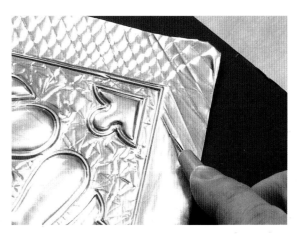

5 Select a background texture (see page 71) and emboss it inside the outer square of the design over a hard work surface (cardboard). Emboss a second background texture outside the square as shown.

6 Apply a paint patina to the finished embossing. Allow the paint to remain only in the deep crevices. Mount the embossing as desired.

Candle Rings

Forget-Me-Not Design

Let this candle ring embossed with flowers and ribbons add even more romance to your candlelit occasions. Its well-defined convex relief and background textures are heightened by applying a black patina.

YOU WILL NEED

Basic tool kit, page 11

Traced pattern, page 75

Aluminum tooling foil, 2 3/4 x 9 inches (7 x 22.9 cm) plus 1-inch-wide (2.5 cm) margins

Food can or jar, 3 inches (7.6 cm) in diameter

String, elastic, or strip of cloth

Candle, 3 inches (7.6 cm) in diameter

TECHNIQUES

Cutting, page 12

Transferring, page 13

Line relief, page 14

Convex relief, page 15

Background relief, page 18

Filling hollows, page 18

Applying a paint patina, page 19

Forget-Me-Not Candle Ring (left);
Simple Grace Candle Ring (right)

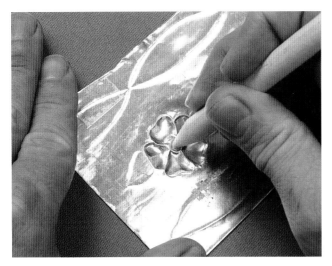

1 Transfer the pattern onto the aluminum tooling foil twice in a row, matching the pattern dots to begin the second transfer. Emboss the flower petals in convex relief. From the front side of the foil, firmly stand the point of the pencil stylus at the base of a petal. Slowly lower the pencil stylus onto the embossed petal to form a crease in the foil. Repeat this technique for each petal in the design. Using a soft work surface (computer mouse pad) and a blending stump, tap and raise the flower centers from the back side of the foil (see photo).

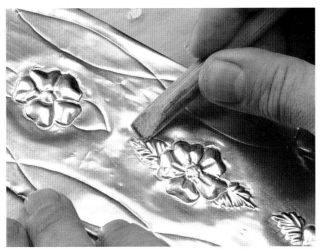

2 From the back side of the foil over a soft work surface (computer mouse pad), emboss lines from the leaf centers to their edges. Working over a very hard work surface (glass pane) define the leaf edges from the front side of the foil. To form a serrated leaf edge, use the corner of a screwdriver stylus and push toward the leaf as you outline (see photo). For a smooth-edged leaf, define the edges with the flat of the screwdriver stylus in a single stroke.

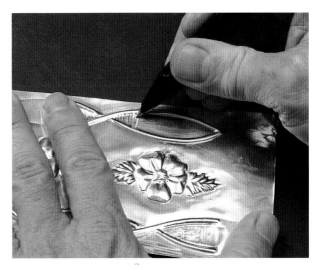

3 Emboss the ribbon edges in line relief. On the front side of the foil, over a hard work surface (cardboard) draw lines across the ribbon with an empty ballpoint pen as shown. Add a background of your choice to the area between the flowers and the ribbon. Fill the hollows. Add a paint patina. Trim the embossed foil at the outer margin of the ribbon.

4 Form the embossed foil strip into a ring by smoothing it around the jar or can. Rub the background with a blending stump (see photo). Glue or tape the ends of the ring around a candle. If gluing, wrap a string, elastic, or cloth strip around the ring until dry.

Candle Rings

Simple Grace Design

Thick copper tooling foil fully supports the embossing of this ornate leaf and vine design. A background of random curly marks adds texture and heightens the metal's shine. Holding the copper over an open flame changes its color, giving it a unique patina.

YOU WILL NEED

Basic tool kit, page 11

Traced pattern, page 75

Thick copper tooling foil, 2 1/2 x 19 1/2 inches (6.4 x 49.5 cm) plus 1-inch-wide (2.5 cm) margins

Transparent drafting ruler

Pliers

Utility lighter

String, elastic, or strip of cloth

Candle, 6 inches (15.2 cm) in diameter

TECHNIQUES

Cutting, page 12

Transferring, page 13

Line relief, page 14

Convex relief, page 15

Background relief, page 18

1 Transfer the pattern onto the thick copper tooling foil. Repeat the pattern down the entire length of the foil by matching the single dot at the end of the pattern to the double dot at the beginning, as shown.

2 Emboss all the lines in line relief, including the center vein of the leaves. Emboss the small circles in convex relief as shown.

3 Working on a soft work surface (computer mouse pad), from the back side of the foil, emboss slightly curved lines from the center veins of the leaves to their edges. Working from the front side of the foil over a soft work surface (computer mouse pad), use a ball stylus to emboss the background of your choice from one edge of the pattern to the other. Working over a very hard work surface (glass pane) with a ball stylus, define the edges of the leaves from the front side of the foil. Push into the design

between the curved lines to form serrated leaf edges as shown. For a smooth-edged leaf, define the edges in a single stroke from the leaf base to its tip.

4 From the back side of the foil place the transparent drafting ruler over the embossed background, 1/8 inch (3 mm) in from the edge of the foil. Use the ball stylus to draw a line down the ruler to begin a fold in the foil. Run the stylus under the edge of the foil while the ruler remains in place to continue the folding process. Remove the ruler and complete the fold with your fingers (see photo).

5 Use pliers to hold the copper embossing over the flame of a utility lighter as shown. Move the embossing over the flame to color the full length of the metal. Wipe off any soot after the copper is cool.

6 Form the strip into a ring by simultaneously pinching both folded edges at 1/2-inch (1.3 cm) intervals. Glue or tape the ends of the ring around the candle. If gluing, wrap a string, elastic, or strip of cloth around the ring until completely dry.

Bird-of-Peace Plaque

A dove bearing an olive branch is a widely recognized symbol representing the renewal of life. In creating this peaceful composition, you will emboss a wide array of interesting forms such as serrated leaves and feathers. Use a subtle background, delicate wing lines, and leaf veins to enhance the tranquil look.

YOU WILL NEED

Basic tool kit, page 11

Traced pattern, page 75

Aluminum tooling foil, 6 x 6 inches (15.2 x 15.2 cm) plus 1-inch-wide (2.5 cm) margins

Hot-glue gun and hot glue

Mounting board, approximately 10 x 10 inches (25.4 x 25.4 cm)

Paper ribbon (optional)

TECHNIQUES

Cutting, page 12

Transferring, page 13

Convex relief, page 15

Flat relief, page 16

Line relief, page 14

Filling hollows, page 18

Background relief, page 18

Applying a paint patina, page 19

Mounting, page 20

BEFORE YOU BEGIN

The leaf and the feather have a similar vein structure. You can make the primary feather shaft and the dominant leaf vein centered, off-centered, or absent altogether. Minor veins may be emphasized highly or given a more subtle appearance. The embossing tool, work surface, and pressure applied combine to determine the style of the stroke. You may choose to emboss these areas either from the center out or from the edges in.

1 Transfer the pattern, and then emboss the head, beak, and upper wings in convex relief as shown.

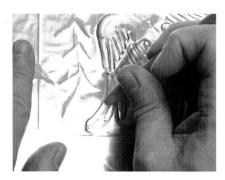

2 Emboss the outer wing feather in flat relief as shown. (Begin with this feather because it overlaps its neighboring feather.) Emboss the next wing feather in flat relief.

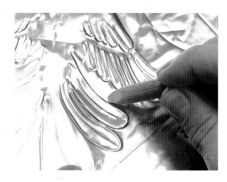

3 Review the feather illustrations above, and select which one or ones you wish to use. Determine where you wish to position the tail feather and primary feather shafts. Form each shaft in line relief. Outline the feathers from the back side of the foil with a pencil stylus, and then define only their outer edges from the front side of the foil with the flat of a screwdriver stylus (see photo).

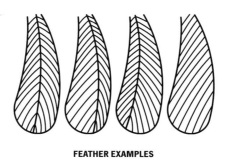

FEATHER EXAMPLES

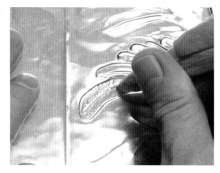

LEAF EXAMPLES

4 On a medium (foam place mat) or hard (cardboard) work surface lightly emboss minor feather veins from the back side of the foil with a pencil stylus.

5 Use line relief to emboss the vine and the leaf veins. Select a leaf shape from the illustrations above, and lightly emboss a leaf around each vein. Emboss the minor leaf veins from the back side of the foil, working

from the center vein to the edges. From the front side of the foil define the outlines with the screwdriver stylus as shown, bottom center. If you wish, use the corner of the screwdriver stylus to form serrations by placing pressure against the outline.

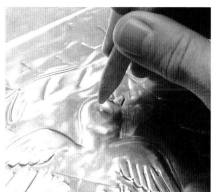

6 Emboss the rest of the bird's body in convex relief. From the front side of the foil, create the bird's eye with a pencil stylus (see photo). Emboss the 6-inch (15.2 cm) square around the image in line relief.

7 Emboss the square as shown with the background of your choice (see page 71 for examples). Fill the hollows; then clean dried filler off the background with a blending stump. Apply a paint patina. Mount your creation on the board of your choice. (I covered a rigid panel with unwrapped, flattened, and overlapped strands of colored paper ribbon, and then centered and adhered the embossing to the paper.)

Renaissance Box

With its classical lines and symmetrical pattern, this design is timeless. By cutting out a simple prong setting, you can inlay a stone, shell, or even a pretty button in the center of the foil. The completed embossing will enhance any flat surface.

YOU WILL NEED

Basic tool kit, page 11

Traced pattern, page 75

Copper tooling foil, 4 x 4 inches (10.2 x 10.2 cm) plus 1-inch-wide (2.5 cm) margins

Stone, must fit in center element of pattern design

Craft box with decorative finish of your choice

TECHNIQUES

Cutting, page 12

Transferring, page 13

Flat relief, page 16

Line relief, page 14

Convex relief, page 15

Background relief, page 18

Filling hollows, page 18

Applying a paint patina, page 19

Mounting, page 20

1 Transfer the pattern onto the copper tooling foil. Determine where the stone will be set in the foil. Scratch the outline of the stone onto the foil with an empty ballpoint pen or ball stylus (see photo, left).

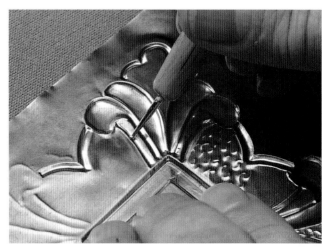

2 The directions below tell you how to plot the prongs to set differently shaped stones into the embossing. The directions are also illustrated on page 47.

Round or Oval Stone

Mark a vertical and a horizontal line across the stone's outline, forming a simple cross. Add a straight line to divide each space in half for a total of eight sections. Mark each line $1/8$ inch (3 mm) in from the stone's outline. The $1/8$-inch (3 mm) lines indicate the end point of the prongs (see photo).

Emerald-shaped Stone

Mark a horizontal line from the farthest left corner to the farthest right corner at the top and bottom of the stone outline. Mark a vertical line from the top left corner to the bottom left corner and from the top right corner to the bottom right corner of the outline. Mark a horizontal line across the center of the stone outline. The sections of the centerline that run between the vertical inner lines and the stone outline indicate the location of the two side prongs. The corner prongs have been formed by the earlier markings.

Square Stone

Mark a vertical and a horizontal centerline across the stone outline to form a cross. Mark each line $1/8$ inch (3 mm) in from each edge of the stone's outline. The $1/8$-inch (3 mm) lines indicate the end point of the prongs.

Odd Shaped Stone

Mark a vertical and a horizontal line across the stone's outline, forming a simple cross. Add a straight line to divide each space in half for a total of eight sections. Mark each line $1/8$ inch (3 mm) in from the stone outline. The $1/8$-inch (3 mm) lines indicate the end point of the prongs.

3 To cut out the V-shaped prongs marked in step 2, place the point of the craft knife blade on the stone outline and $1/16$ inch (1.6 mm) outside the prong mark. Cut the foil straight to the tip of the prong line. Repeat this process to cut the other side of the prong. Cut out the other prongs marked in step 2. Smooth the prong setting toward its center with a screwdriver stylus over a very hard work surface (glass pane). Use flat relief to emboss the square shape at the center of the pattern design. Emboss the curved lines in line relief (see photo).

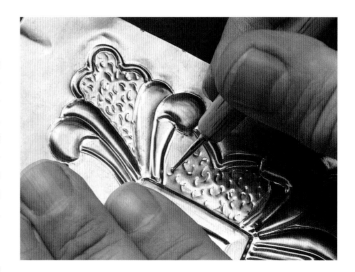

4 Emboss the remainder of the design in convex relief. Emboss a background design of your choice between the relief sections as shown.

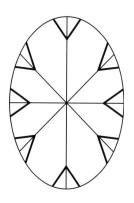

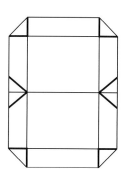

5 Fill the hollows and apply a paint patina. Cut out the embossed foil as shown. Place the image face up on a hard work surface (cardboard). Use an upright ball stylus to rub under all sharp edges.

Plotting prongs on a round or oval stone

Plotting prongs on an emerald-shaped stone

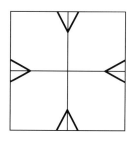

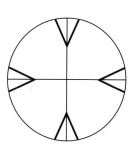

6 Firmly hold a plastic card at the base of each prong and raise the prong tip with the point of the craft knife blade as shown. Use clear-drying glue to adhere the stone to the center of the setting and the prongs to the stone.

Plotting prongs on a square stone

Plotting prongs on a small circle stone

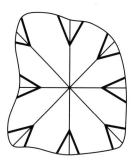

7 Smooth the prongs onto the stone with a screwdriver stylus as shown. Clean off any excess glue with a damp cloth. Mount the remainder of the embossing to the box top.

Plotting prongs on an odd-shaped stone

On-the-Vine Wine Basket

This handy and attractive tote will let you carry picnic supplies or present party gifts in style. Four copper foil pieces are individually embossed, separately cut out, and then artfully arranged. A patina solution provides the perfect finish for the leaves, and a copper wire makes lovely spiral tendrils.

YOU WILL NEED

Basic tool kit, page 11

Thick copper tooling foil, 4 x 3 inches (10.2 x 7.6 cm) plus 1-inch-wide (2.5 cm) margins

3 thick copper tooling foil pieces, each 3 ½ x 2 ½ inches (8.9 x 6.4 cm) plus 1-inch-wide (2.5 cm) margins

Traced patterns, page 76

Plastic circle template

Liquid patina solution, green

Small paintbrush

3 pieces 20-gauge copper wire, each 4 inches (10.2 cm)

Wire cutters

Hot-glue gun and hot glue

Basket of your choice

TECHNIQUES

Cutting, page 12

Transferring, page 13

Line relief, page 14

Convex relief, page 15

Filling hollows, page 18

Applying a liquid patina, page 19

Mounting, page 20

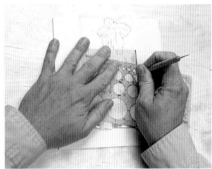

1 Transfer the patterns onto the tooling foil, using a circle template as needed (see photo). Use the back and front sides of the pattern to transfer the three leaves.

2 Form the major veins of the leaves in line relief. Emboss the leaf edges from the back side of the foil over a soft work surface (computer mouse pad) as shown. Use one corner of the screwdriver stylus as you keep the other corner off and over the leaf image.

3 Work on the front side of each leaf over a very hard work surface (glass pane) with a ball stylus. Firmly push in the leaf outline at random points to create unique edges and creases (see photo). Return to the back side of the foil, and lightly emboss angled lines from the vein to the tip of each leaf.

4 Emboss the back of each grape in a circular as well as a rocking motion on a soft work surface (computer mouse pad). Work with an extra-broad pencil

stylus, and then a broad blending stump. Turn the foil over and use a very hard work surface (glass pane). Select a circle template that is large enough to allow a small ball stylus to retrace the grape outline and define the edge (see photo, bottom left). Repeat this step for each grape until the desired relief is obtained.

5 Place the embossed grape cluster on a very soft work surface (foam rubber) or in your hand. Use a wide blending stump or soft cloth to curve the cluster (see photo). On the front side of the foil, over a very hard work surface (glass pane), flatten the outer edge of the cluster with a screwdriver stylus, and then outline it with a ball stylus. Following the manufacturer's instructions, color the leaves by applying the green liquid patina solution.

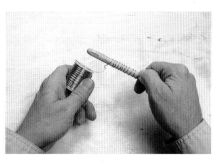

6 To make the wire tendrils, form a small ¼-inch (6 mm) triangle at one end of a 4-inch (10.2 cm) piece of the copper wire. Coil the rest of the wire around a pencil or stylus as shown. Remove the wire and slightly stretch it to separate the coils. Repeat this process to create additional tendrils.

7 Fill the grape cluster's hollows to maintain and support its curved form. Keep in mind that the outer edges of the cluster will need to come in contact with the mounting surface. Fill the hollows of the leaves (see photo). For more dimension when mounted, add more filler in any one area of each leaf.

8 Cut out the embossed pieces as shown. Place each face up on a hard work surface (cardboard), and push their edges slightly under with an upright ball stylus. Arrange the pieces in an artful manner and adhere them to the basket with hot glue. Sections of the leaves may be mounted under the grape cluster. Insert the triangle end of the copper-wire tendrils under any embossed piece.

Fruit-of-the-Earth Journal Cover

Family album, bridal register, address book, or journal—all become more special with a handmade cover. On this one-of-a-kind embossing, bold wheat stalks are created in high and heavily defined convex relief. Two backgrounds surround the design; one is low and light, while one is deep and heavy. Woven strips of contrasting metals complete the composition.

YOU WILL NEED

Basic tool kit, page 11

Spiral-bound journal or blank book, 8 1/2 x 6 inches (21.6 x 15.2 cm)

Traced jacket pattern, page 78

2 aluminum tooling foil sheets, each 10 x 12 1/2 inches (25.4 x 31.8 cm)

Traced design pattern, page 76

Brass tooling foil, 1 x 6 inches (2.5 x 15.2 cm)

Copper tooling foil, 1 x 4 inches (2.5 x 10.2 cm)

Aluminum tooling foil, 6 x 8 inches (15.2 x 20.3 cm)

Pinking shears

TECHNIQUES

Cutting, page 12

Transferring, page 13

Line relief, page 14

Background relief, page 18

Filling hollows, page 18

Applying a paint patina, page 19

Mounting, page 20

1 Carefully remove the front and rear book covers from the wire spiral. Using the jacket pattern, transfer and cut out two aluminum foil covers. Mark the fold on the spiral side of the flap onto both foil covers. With the spiral side of one cover on the left, center and transfer the design pattern onto the foil.

2 Emboss the stems in line relief. Without raising the pencil stylus, emboss each wheat grain from the tip to the bottom, and back to the tip. Outline each grain from the front side of the foil on a very hard work surface (glass pane) with a pencil stylus as shown. Repeat this process in sequence for each grain. Add a ½-inch-wide (1.3 cm) low-relief background around the entire wheat design.

3 Fill the hollows, adding more filler at the center of each wheat head as shown. Let dry. Cut horizontal slits on the foil at the lines marked on the photocopied design pattern. On a hard work surface (cardboard) emboss the remainder of the front aluminum book cover and all of the back aluminum book cover with a background pattern of your choice.

4 Trim the width of the copper and brass foil strips to fit through the slits cut in step 3. Clip the corners of one end of each strip at an angle. Weave the strips through the slits (see photo). Fold back the strip ends under the book cover.

5 Apply an even layer of glue to the back side of the front book cover's spiral-side flap. Align and adhere the foil to the spiral-side edge of the book's inside front flap. Smooth the foil with a blending stump to remove air bubbles and to locate the holes (see photo). Repeat the process to partially adhere the other cover.

6 Place a book cover with the spiral flap up, on a soft work surface (computer mouse pad). Use the tip of a craft knife to cut slits in the foil from the center to the sides of the spiral holes. With a ball stylus, push the slit foil into the holes, and shape the openings (see photo, bottom center).

7 Apply an even layer of glue to the remainder of the aluminum foil book cover. Firmly hold the adhered foil flap and book cover on a very hard work surface (glass pane). Slowly drag and turn them around to the other side as shown. Rub the outer cover with a wadded cloth from the folded edge to the opposite side. Fold and adhere the other flaps using the same drag-and-turn process.

8 From the inside of the foil-covered flap, mark the center of each spiral hole with a dot. Slit and shape the holes from the front of the book as described in step 6. Use pinking shears to cut two aluminum tooling foil rectangles, each a little larger than the uncovered area on the inside of the book cover. Adhere the rectangles to the book cover as shown. Add a patina to both sides of the foil covers. Reinstall the covers onto the wire spiral. Write your name or a dedication on the inside covers with an empty ballpoint pen if you wish.

Splendor-of-the-Season Watering Can

The blooming tulips of spring look especially elegant in high relief. This thick copper gardenscape transforms an ordinary aluminum watering can into a work of art. The background texture is a prominent basket weave, and the green patina is achieved with a liquid solution.

YOU WILL NEED

Basic tool kit, page 11

Thick copper tooling foil,
5 x 5 3/4 inches (12.7 x
14.6 cm) plus 1-inch-wide
(2.5 cm) margins

Traced pattern, page 76

Liquid patina solution, green

Small paintbrush

Aluminum watering can

TECHNIQUES

Cutting, page 12

Transferring, page 13

Line relief, page 14

Convex relief, page 15

Filling hollows, page 18

Background relief, page 18

Applying a paint patina,
page 19

Mounting, page 20

1 Transfer the pattern onto the thick copper tooling foil as shown.

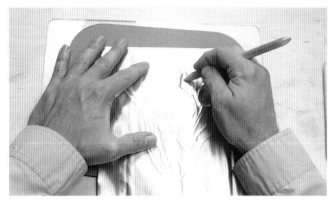

2 Use convex relief to emboss each tulip, fully completing one petal at a time.

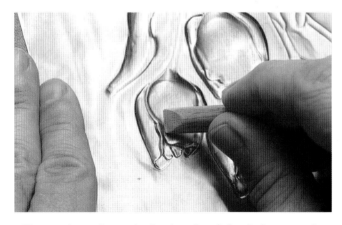

3 Working from the back side of the foil on a soft work surface (computer mouse pad), use a screwdriver stylus to retrace only the upper part of the petals (see photo). Apply pressure only on the corner of the screwdriver stylus that is outlining the petal. This gives each flower a more natural appearance. Working from the front side of the foil, finish each petal's outline with the ball stylus.

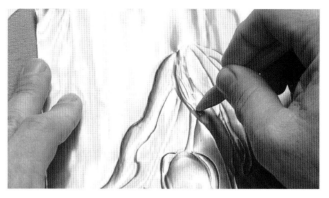

4 Emboss the stems and leaves in convex relief to create a natural appearance as shown. Fill the hollows.

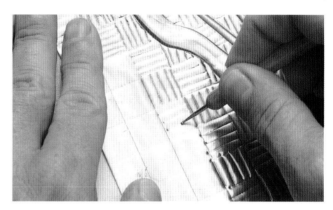

5 From the front side of the foil on a very hard work surface (glass pane) use a blending stump to smooth the background flat. Use a ball stylus on the front side of the foil to add vertical and horizontal lines to the background at ½-inch (1.3 cm) intervals. Draw closely packed lines within the squares to form a basketweave pattern (see photo).

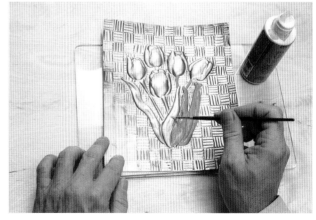

6 Add a paint patina. Following the manufacturer's instructions, add the liquid patina solution to the stems and leaves of the tulips. The solution gives the copper its green color. Use a hot-glue gun and hot glue to mount the embossing on an aluminum watering can.

Wandering Zebras

Zebras are a fitting subject for a bold line-relief embossing. Their white stripes are the high peaks of the metal; their dark stripes recede far into the background, thanks to a black paint patina. Add a natural savannah-like setting in which the zebras can roam, and you will have a very scenic embossing.

1 Transfer the pattern onto the aluminum tooling foil. Completely emboss each zebra stripe and each grass blade in line relief before starting another relief line. Using a dry ballpoint pen or a wooden skewer is helpful for embossing very narrow lines (see photo). Emboss the tree leaves in line relief with a broad pencil stylus.

2 From the front side of the foil, over a very hard work surface (glass pane), flatten the recessed area between the stripes and leaves by making a tight spiraling motion with a dry ballpoint pen as shown.

3 Use a pencil stylus to fill the background with the same spiraling pattern (see photo). The change in embossing tools slightly alters the appearance of the line, but the zebras will still blend in with their background.

4 Contour the zebra bodies in convex relief. Use a broad blending stump over a very soft work surface (foam rubber). You may prefer to hold the foil in the palm of your hand as shown and use a cloth-wrapped thumb to rub the back side of the image. Do not raise the ears and mane.

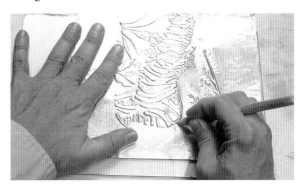

5 From the front side of the foil on a very hard work surface (glass pane), use a pencil stylus to outline the outer edges of the zebra bodies, excluding the ears and mane. Repeat steps 4 and 5 as many times as needed to achieve the amount of relief you desire.

6 Hold the embossing in your hand and fill the hollows. Let dry. Add a paint patina to the front surface. Remove as little of the black medium as possible from the recessed areas and the background. For greater contrast, immediately polish the raised stripes with a soft cloth as shown. Mount and frame the embossing as desired. (This eye-catching faux zebra skin mat and shiny red metal frame show just how wild wildlife scenes can be!)

Macramé Mirror Frame

The distinctive brass embossings applied to this mirror feature an intricate knot motif representing the unity that binds together friends and family. As you create numerous sweeping curves, you will gain plenty of experience embossing in flat relief. The frame is a solid sheet of foil cleverly slit at the corners to hold a photograph.

YOU WILL NEED

Basic tool kit, page 11

Mirror, 8 x 10 inches (20.3 x 25.4 cm)

Tempered hardwood, 8 x 10 inches (20.3 x 25.4 cm)

Clothespins

Traced patterns A and B, pages 77 and 78

Plastic circle template or two coins (one 1 inch [2.5 cm] and one 3/4 inch [1.9 cm] in diameter)

Thin brass tooling foil, 6 x 7 1/2 inches (15.2 x 19 cm) plus 1-inch-wide (2.5 cm) margins

4 thin brass tooling foil strips, each 1 3/4 x 5 inches (4.4 x 12.7 cm) plus 1-inch-wide (2.5 cm) margins

4 thin brass tooling foil strips, each 1 x 7 inches (2.5 x 17.8 cm) plus 1-inch-wide (2.5 cm) margins

Transparent drafting ruler

Transparent acetate sheet, 3 x 5 inches (7.6 x 12.7 cm)

TECHNIQUES

Cutting, page 12

Transferring, page 13

Flat relief, page 16

Background relief, page 18

Filling hollows, page 18

Applying a paint patina, page 19

Mounting, page 20

BEFORE YOU BEGIN

Use circle templates or coins to guide the stylus along the curves. Use the large coin to steer the stylus around the outside curves and the small one for the inside curves. These circle guides are not the exact size, so you will need to frequently adjust their position. A plastic card will be handy for creating the short straight lines.

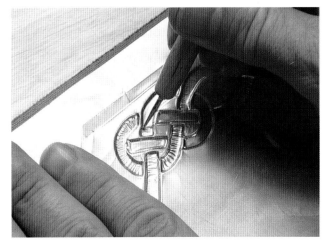

1 Glue the tempered hardwood to the back side of the mirror. Secure the pieces together with clothespins and let dry. Transfer pattern A (the frame centerpiece) onto the large piece of thin brass tooling foil. Transfer pattern B (the corner design) onto four of the small brass tooling foil strips. Emboss all the pieces in flat relief. Add lines across the ribbon images from the back side of the foil to add background texture as shown.

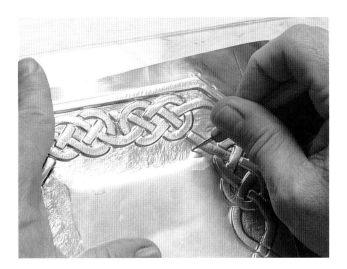

2 Add a low relief background from the edges of the frame centerpiece to the center of the rectangle, covering about 1 ½ inches (3.8 cm) on all sides (see photo).

3 Use a craft knife to make slits at the four dash lines shown on the inside corners of pattern A. Insert the knife into the slits and widen the space to hold the corners of a photograph and the protective acetate film (see photo).

4 Fill the hollows of all the embossed pieces. Add a paint patina. Cut out the outer edge of the frame centerpiece and the four foil corners as shown. Place the embossed pieces face up on a hard work surface (cardboard). Rub the sharp edges under with an upright ball stylus.

5 Center an embossed foil corner on a corner of the board-backed mirror. Fold the edges of the foil back to cover the mirror corner. Use the side of a stylus to shape the foil corner to fit the mirror corner as shown. Remove the foil corner, and then shape the other three foil corners using the same technique.

7 On a medium work surface (foam place mat) use a ball stylus and a drafting ruler to draw a line along the length of one thin foil strip, $1/4$ inch (6 mm) in from its edge. Continue to hold the ruler on the line and run the point of a pencil stylus under the foil edge until it folds upward. Place the mirror edge over the $1/4$-inch (6 mm) fold. Use the side of a stylus to mold the folded foil strip to the mirror (see photo). Remove this folded foil edge wrap, and then form the other three.

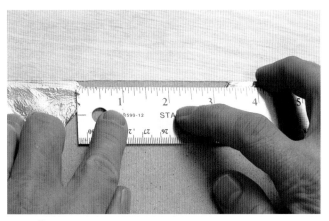

6 With two adjacent foil corners temporarily in place, measure the distance of the uncovered mirror edge between them as shown, and add $1/2$ inch (1.3 cm). Cut a strip of thin brass tooling foil to this measurement. Repeat this process for the other edges of the mirror.

8 Apply glue to all the embossed pieces and edge wraps except the areas near the photo slits. Adhere the edge wraps, the corners, and then the centerpiece to the mirror. Position rubber bands along the edges to hold the corners while they dry. Place a piece of soft foam rubber and a heavy book over the centerpiece. After the glue dries, insert a $3 1/2$ x 5-inch (8.9 x 12.7 cm) photo and acetate sheet into the slits as shown.

Aztec Sun Tile

The sun, revered in ancient cultures, is a powerful symbol of life and growth. In this embossing, the warm tones of brass convey the sun's heat, and the broad convex relief lets the metallic surface reflect an abundance of light. A golden paint, specifically designed for use on metal, provides additional highlights.

YOU WILL NEED

Basic tool kit, page 11

Traced pattern, page 77

Thin brass tooling foil, 6 1/4 x 6 1/4 inches (15.9 x 15.9 cm) plus 1-inch-wide (2.5 cm) margins

Gold paint for metal

Paintbrush

Ceramic tile, 6 x 6 inches (15.2 x 15.2 cm)

Metal crimper (optional)

4 thin copper tooling foil strips, each 1/2 x 6 inches (15.2 x 1.3 cm) (optional)

Decorative metal studs (optional)

TECHNIQUES

Cutting, page 12

Transferring, page 13

Line relief, page 14

Convex relief, page 15

Concave relief, page 15

Filling hollows, page 18

Applying a paint patina, page 19

Mounting, page 20

BEFORE YOU BEGIN

Unlike most embossing projects, the standard principle of working from the center to the edges does not apply to the Aztec Sun Tile. Because the sun's face has a high convex relief, you will emboss it after the sun rays to prevent damage.

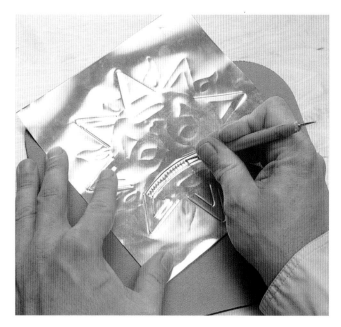

1 Transfer the pattern onto the thin brass tooling foil. Emboss all the straight-line sun rays and the sun's headband in line relief (see photo).

2 Emboss the center area of the straight-line rays and the flame-shaped rays in convex relief. From the front side of the foil on a very hard work surface (glass pane), use a small ball stylus to flatten the center of the flame rays as shown.

3 Use your finger as a work surface to emboss the sun's face and head as shown. Alternate from one feature to another in convex and concave relief.

4 Fill the hollows while holding the embossing in a cupped hand. Leave the centers of the flame rays free of filler. Place the embossing over a bowl to dry so the sun's facial features will not flatten (see photo). If needed, refill hollows.

5 Neatly and carefully cut out the embossed sun from the brass foil, and then cut out the centers of the flame rays as shown.

6 Place the sun face up over a hard work surface (cardboard). Hold a ball stylus upright and rub the sharp edges of the cut foil under as shown.

7 Add a paint patina, and then paint the flame rays and the head and cheek decorations with gold metallic paint as shown. Mount the embossing on the 6 x 6-inch (15.2 x 15.2 cm) tile with a heavy-duty clear-drying glue.

8 If desired, run the four ½ x 6-inch (15.2 x 1.3 cm) strips of thin copper foil through a metal crimper as shown. Attach the crimped strips and the decorative studs to the edges of the tile with a heavy-duty clear-drying glue.

Daisy Chain Frame

Embossing this frame petal by petal, and leaf by leaf is like watching your garden bloom. The domed shapes of convex forms radiate incredible lustre. A black paint patina worked deep into the frame's recesses provides dramatic contrast, and a border of decorative aluminum strips completes the composition.

YOU WILL NEED

Basic tool kit, page 11

Traced pattern, page 78

Aluminum tooling foil, 6 ¹/₂ x 8 ¹/₂ inches (16.5 x 21.6 cm) plus 1-inch-wide (2.5 cm) margins

2 aluminum tooling foil strips, each 1 x 10 ¹/₂ inches (2.5 x 26.7 cm)

2 aluminum tooling foil strips, each 1 x 8 ¹/₂ inches (2.5 x 21.6 cm)

Transparent drafting ruler

Decorator scissors

Glass pane, 8 x 10 inches (20.3 x 25.4 cm)

Commercial easel back

Adhesive-backed hook-and-loop fasteners

TECHNIQUES

Cutting, page 12

Transferring, page 13

Line relief, page 14

Convex relief, page 15

Background relief, page 18

Filling hollows, page 18

Adding a paint patina, page 19

Mounting, page 20

1 Transfer the pattern onto the large piece of aluminum tooling foil. Working from the back side of the foil on a soft work surface (computer mouse pad), use a pencil stylus to give each petal a ruffled contour. Emboss long random strokes from the base to the edges as shown. Define the boundary of each petal from the front side of the foil with a pencil stylus over a very hard work surface (glass pane).

3 Use convex relief to emboss a leaf section so it appears to curl up as shown. From the back side of the foil, outline the upper part of this section with the corner of the screwdriver stylus. Outline the rest of the leaf from the back side of the foil. Further define the whole leaf from the front side of the foil with a pencil stylus. Draw the leaf veins from the front side of the foil. Use this technique to emboss the other leaves.

2 Emboss the flower bud and stem structures in convex relief. Working on a soft work surface (computer mouse pad), tap randomly at the center of each flower with a pencil stylus from the back side of the foil. From the front side of the foil on a very hard work surface (glass pane), outline the center of the flowers with a pencil stylus as shown.

4 On the front side of the foil over a very hard work surface (glass pane), use a small ball stylus to draw tight scribbles in the spaces between the foliage (see photo).

5 Fill the hollows, and then add a paint patina. Cut out the interior and exterior edges of the embossed design. Place the embossing face up on a hard work surface (cardboard) and use an upright ball stylus to rub under the sharp cut edges as shown.

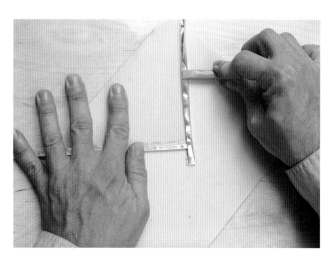

7 Place the decorative edge of the foil strip under the glass pane. Fold and flatten the strip around the edge of the glass with a screwdriver stylus (see photo). Remove the foil edge wrap from the glass. Use this process to shape the other three foil edge wraps.

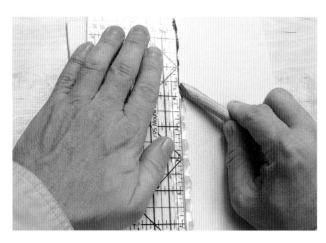

6 Cut one long edge of a foil strip with decorator scissors. On a medium work surface (foam place mat) use a drafting ruler to draw a line along the length of and 1/4 inch (6 mm) inside the decorative edge. Place the same ruler 1/2 inch (1.3 cm) in from the decorated edge, and cut the foil at this point with a craft knife. Position and firmly hold the ruler at the fold. Run the point of a pencil stylus back and forth under the foil until it folds up against the ruler (see photo). Repeat this step on the other three aluminum tooling foil strips.

8 Slightly widen one of the shorter foil edge wraps, and brush glue inside. Adhere this wrap to a short glass edge. Use a pencil stylus to remove air bubbles and excess glue from under the foil. Immediately clean the edges of the glass with a damp cloth. Adhere the second short wrap on the opposite short side of the glass. Hold the foil edge wraps in place with rubber bands until the glue is dry. Apply the last two, longer foil edge wraps to the longer glass edges, and then cut off the protruding ends as shown. Adhere the embossed daisy frame onto the center of the glass, and let dry. Attach the purchased easel back to the frame with adhesive-backed hook-and-loop fasteners.

Basket of Love

Calligraphy is one of the most expressive art forms. This Asian character for love symbolizes an enduring, cherished, and loving friendship. In this design, the central image is embossed in flat relief while the bamboo-like border is created in line relief. The regal shimmer of the brass foil is in harmony with the classical lines of the dark woven basket on which it is mounted.

YOU WILL NEED

Basic tool kit, page 11

Traced pattern, page 78

Thin brass tooling foil,
5 1/2 x 7 1/2 inches
(14 x 19 cm) plus 1-inch-wide
(2.5 cm) margins

Transparent drafting ruler

Flat-walled basket, large
enough to accommodate
embossing (optional)

4 brass brads (optional)

TECHNIQUES

Cutting, page 12

Transferring, page 13

Line relief, page 14

Flat relief, page 16

Background relief, page 18

Filling hollows, page 18

Applying a paint patina,
page 19

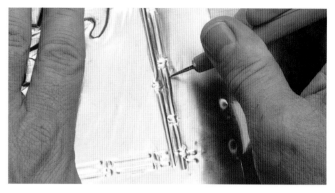

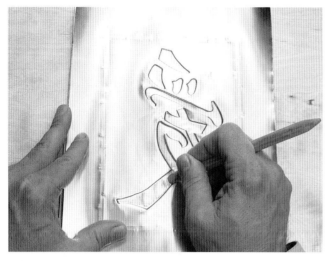

1 Transfer the pattern onto the center of the tooling foil. Emboss the central character in flat relief.

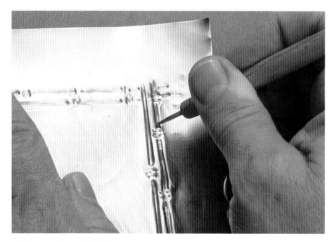

2 From the back side of the foil, apply a subtle fabric texture to the central character by drawing very close vertical and horizontal lines with an empty ballpoint pen on a very hard work surface (glass pane).

3 Emboss the long and short lines that form the bamboo frame with a wide ball stylus from the back side of the foil over a soft work surface (computer mouse pad).

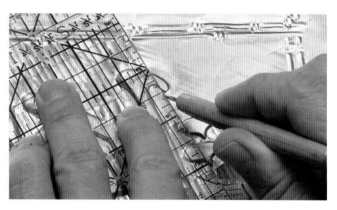

4 From the front side of the foil on a very hard work surface (glass pane), use a small ball stylus to define only the outer edges of the bamboo sticks (see photo). Make the centers of the longer bamboo sections slightly narrower. Fill the hollows of the embossing.

5 Add a background pattern that resembles a bamboo mat. From the front side of the foil over a soft work surface (computer mouse pad), use a medium ball stylus and a transparent drafting ruler to draw closely packed lines as shown. From the back side of the foil draw perpendicular lines to those previously drawn at $1/2$-inch (1.3 cm) intervals.

6 Apply a paint patina to the embossing. If desired, mount it to the basket with brass brads at the corners (see photo).

GALLERY

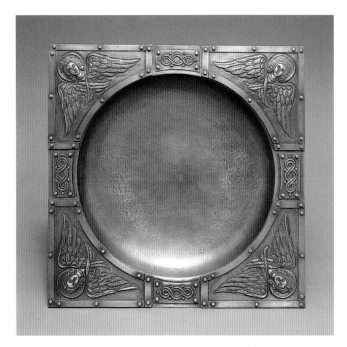

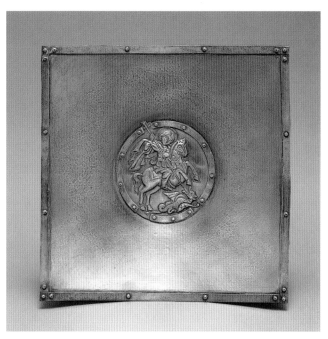

Valentin Yotkov. *Collections Plate*, 1999. 12 x 12 x 1 1/4 in. (30.5 x 30.5 x 3.2 cm). Raised copper, patina, beeswax; repoussé. Photo by Plamen Petkov

Valentin Yotkov. *Collections Plate III*, 1999. 11 1/4 x 3 in. (28.6 x 7.6 cm). Raised copper, patina, beeswax; repoussé. Photo by Plamen Petkov

Valentin Yotkov. *Bowl*, 1999. 3 x 4 3/4 in. (7.6 x 12.1 cm). Sterling silver; fabricated, chased. Photo by Plamen Petkov

Valentin Yotkov. *Vase*, 1999. 12 1/4 x 5 1/4 in. (31.1 x 13.3 cm). Copper, patina, beeswax; chased and raised.
Photo by Plamen Petkov

Laura Taylor. *Sweet Dreams Clock*, 2002. 11 ¹/₂ x 8 ¹/₂ x 1 in. (29.2 x 21.6 x 2.5 cm). Aluminum tooling foil, wood; metal embossing. Photo by artist

Laura Taylor. *Celebrate Gift Tag*, 2002. 3 ¹/₂ x 6 in. (8.9 x 15.2 cm). Brass tooling foil; metal embossing. Photo by artist

Teri Blond. *Dutch Girl* (detail), 1998. 11 ¹/₂ x 3 ¹/₂ x 1 in. (29.2 x 8.9 x 2.5 cm) neck piece with chain. Recycled sterling silver repoussé spoon-bowl, seashell back, sterling silver bezel, sterling silver wire, fresh-water pearls, sterling silver handle, agate, sterling candle holder base, blued hanger wire chain; mixed media construction. Photo by Bobby Hansson

Teri Blond. *Ruby-Jargoon* (detail), 1998. 11 ¹/₂ x 4 ¹/₂ x ³/₄ in. (29.2 x 11.4 x 1.9 cm) overall with chain. Recycled embossed sterling silver hair brush handle, copper foil, wood base, sterling wire, foil-backed stones, seed pearls, star ruby, black pearls, handmade sterling chain; mixed media construction. Photo by Harry Geyer

Teri Blond. *Blue Madonna*, 2001. 6 x 8 ¹/₂ x ¹/₂ in. (15.2 x 21.6 x 1.3 cm). Embossed pewter, glass opal, glass half-pearls, hand-painted faces and a faux-finished jigsaw frame; mixed media construction. Photo by Holly Turner

Linda Greenway. *Cat Watching Pond*, 2000. 8 x 19 in. (20.3 x 48.3 cm). Copper; metal embossing. Photo by Larry Sanders

Linda Greenway. *Hummingbirds and Trumpet Vine*, 2000. 10 in. (25.4 cm) in diameter. Copper; metal embossing. Photo by Larry Sanders

Linda Greenway. *Wetland with Egrets*, 2000. 8 x 19 in. (20.3 x 48.3 cm). Copper; metal embossing. Photo by Larry Sanders

Linda Greenway. *Koi*, 2000. 10 in. (25.4 cm) in diameter. Copper; metal embossing. Photo by Larry Sanders

Yolanda Carranza Valle. *Torie's Treasures*, 2001. 7 1/4 x 5 x 3 1/2 in. (18.4 x 12.7 x 8.9 cm). Aluminum, wooden box; metal embossing. Photo by Evan Bracken

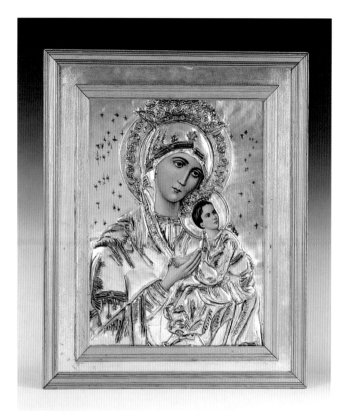

Yolanda Carranza Valle. *Madonna Icon*, 1998. 14 x 21 in. (35.6 x 53.3 cm). Aluminum, reproduced painting, wooden frame; metal embossing. Photo by Evan Bracken

Yolanda Carranza Valle. *Pharaoh*, 2000. 7 x 9 in. (17.8 x 22.9 cm). Aluminum, wooden base; metal embossing. Photo by Evan Bracken

Yolanda Carranza Valle. *Radiant Energy*, 2002. 15 1/2 x 19 1/2 in. (39.4 x 49.5 cm). Aluminum, brass, copper, wooden tray; woven metal, metal embossing. Photo by Evan Bracken

Yolanda Carranza Valle. *Kachina Rhythm*, 1999. 6 x 6 in. (15.2 x 15.2 cm). Aluminum, tile, striated quartz; metal embossing and inlay. Photo by Evan Bracken

BACKGROUND TEXTURES

1. Flying Commas

2. Dancing Crosses

3. Baby Locks

4. Thatch

5. Rose

6. Basket Weave

7. Snow Fall

8. Lattice

9. Linen

10. Drizzle

11. Mosaic

12. Bubbles

13. Cobweb

14. Loopty Loop

15. Spiral

TEMPLATES

Sampler, page 22 (enlarge 150%)

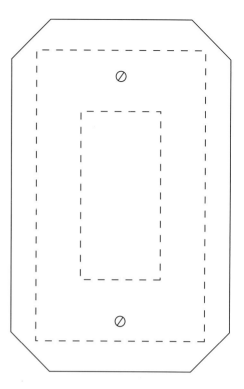

Switch Covers, page 24
Base template: decorator base
(enlarge 150%)

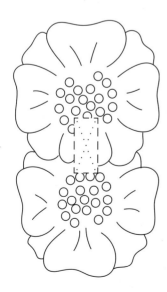

Switch Covers, page 24
Spring (enlarge 150%)

Switch Covers, page 24
Lace (enlarge 150%)

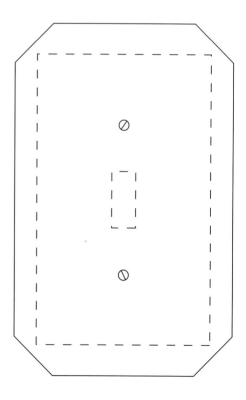

Switch Covers, page 24
Base template: toggle switch
(enlarge 150%)

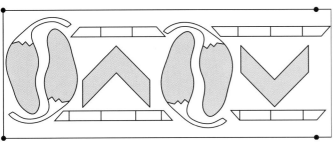

Chili Pepper Bottle, page 29, Pattern A

Chili Pepper Bottle, page 29
Pattern B (enlarge 150%)

Chili Pepper Bottle, page 29
Pattern C

Switch Covers, page 24
Hunter's Pride (enlarge 150%)

Switch Covers, page 24
Desert Friends (enlarge 150%)

Catch-of-the-Day Panel, page 27
Fish 1 (enlarge 125%)

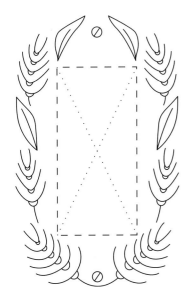

Switch Covers, page 24
Harvest (enlarge 150%)

Catch-of-the-Day Panel, page 27
Fish 2 (enlarge 125%)

Bear Tracks Panel, page 31
(enlarge 150%)

Beautiful Book Trimming, page 33
Pattern A, medallion design
(enlarge 125%)

Beautiful Book Trimming, page 33
Pattern B, single flower design

Butterfly Basket, page 36
(enlarge 150%)

Moroccan Medallion, page 38 (enlarge 200%)

Bird-of-Peace Plaque, page 43 (enlarge 200%)

Forget-Me-Not Candle Ring, page 40 (enlarge 150%)

Renaissance Box, page 45
Embossing Template
(enlarge 125%)

Simple Grace Candle Ring, page 42 (enlarge 125%)

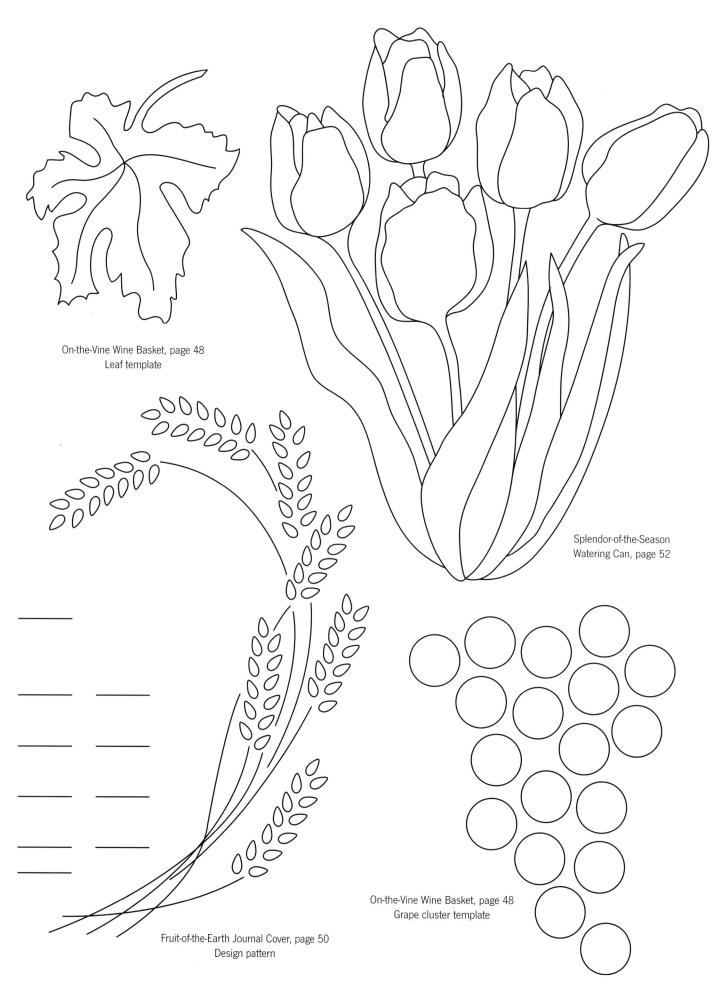

On-the-Vine Wine Basket, page 48
Leaf template

Splendor-of-the-Season
Watering Can, page 52

Fruit-of-the-Earth Journal Cover, page 50
Design pattern

On-the-Vine Wine Basket, page 48
Grape cluster template

Fruit-of-the-Earth Journal Cover, page 50
Jacket pattern (enlarge 200%)

Aztec Sun Tile, page 59
(enlarge 150%)

Wandering Zebras, page 54

Daisy Chain Frame, page 62
(enlarge 150%)

Basket of Love, page 65
(enlarge 200%)

Macramé Mirror, page 56
Pattern B (corner design)
(enlarge 125%)

Macramé Mirror Frame, page 56
Pattern A (frame centerpiece)
(enlarge 200%)

ABOUT THE AUTHOR

 In 1994, Yolanda Valle's inquisitive nature led her to pursue metal embossing. Finding little written material on the subject, she sought out a practicing master artisan from Mexico who was willing to share her skills. After years of experimentation, practice, and refinement, Yolanda developed her own original embossing techniques and patterns. She has exhibited her artwork in boutiques and galleries, The Selena Auditorium, and The Art Museum of South Texas in Corpus Christi, Texas.

Yolanda Valle has a masters degree in secondary education with certification in the fields of biology, geography, and life and earth sciences. She taught earth science for 31 years in the Taft Independent School District in Taft, Texas.

NOTES ON SUPPLIERS

Usually, the supplies you need for making the projects in Lark books can be found at your local craft supply store, discount mart, home improvement center, or retail shop relevant to the topic of the book. Occasionally, however, you may need to buy materials or tools from specialty suppliers. In order to provide you with the most up-to-date information, we have created a listing of suppliers on our Web site, which we update on a regular basis. Visit us at www.larkbooks.com, click on "Craft Supply Sources," and then click on the relevant topic. You will find numerous companies listed with their web address and/or mailing address and phone number.

ACKNOWLEDGMENTS

I would like to dedicate this book to Hector Valle, my best friend and husband, and to our children, Gery, Gabe, Evelyn, Laura, Crystal, Carrie, and Terrie.

Thanks also to:
Susan Davis, grammar police and colleague, whose kind and patient advice guided me in writing.

Eduvijes Carranza, my titlesmith and mother, whose imagination took charge of naming the projects.

Daniel Carranza, my computer guru and brother, whose expertise piloted me toward computer skills.

All of the talented artists who contributed images of their repoussé and metal embossings to the gallery. Thank you for sharing your unique and inspiring photographs.

INDEX

Alloy, 7
Anneal, 7
Applying a paint patina, 19
Background textures, 71
Background relief, 18
Basic tool kit, 11
Blending stumps, 10
Broad pencil stylus, 10
Comfort, 21
Commercial patina solutions, 10
Common thickness labels, 7
Concave relief, 15
Convex relief, 15
Craft knives, 9
Cutting circles and curves, 12
Cutting straight lines, 12
Cutting surfaces, 9
Cutting tools, 9
Cutting with a craft knife, 12
Embossing, 6
Embossing tools, 9
Extra-broad pencil stylus, 10
Filling the hollows, 18
Filling tools, 10
Fine-point pencil stylus, 10
Flat relief, 16
Gauge, 7
Glues, 11
Hollows, 10
Lighting, 21
Line relief, 14

Metal ball stylus, 10
Metal foil thickness, 7
Metal ruler, 9
Metal tooling foils, 7
Metric, 7
Mils, 7
Mounting tools, 11
Mounting with adhesives, 20
Paint patinas, 11
Patina, 10
Patina supplies, 10
Pencil styluses, 10
Plastic cards, 9
Plastic circle template, 9
Relief, 6
Repoussé, 21
Safety, 21
Scissors, 9
Scoring, 12
Screwdriver styluses, 10
Sharpening knife blades, 9
Sharpening stone, 9
Techniques, 12
Tooling, 7
Transferring a design, 13
Transferring tools, 8
Upfold, 14
Using tracing paper, 13
Wood filler, 10
Wooden styluses, 10
Work surfaces, 8